BARBARA BUSH

THE CHELSEA HOUSE LIBRARY OF BIOGRAPHY

BARBARA BUSH

ARLENE McGRATH HEISS

Chelsea House Publishers

New York • Philadelphia

CHELSEA HOUSE PUBLISHERS

EDITOR-IN-CHIEF Remmel Nunn
MANAGING EDITOR Karyn Gullen Browne
COPY CHIEF Mark Rifkin
PICTURE EDITOR Adrian Allen
ART DIRECTOR Maria Epes
ASSISTANT ART DIRECTOR Noreen Romano
MANUFACTURING DIRECTOR Gerald Levine
SYSTEMS MANAGER Lindsey Ottman
PRODUCTION MANAGER Joseph Romano
PRODUCTION COORDINATOR Marie Claire Cebrián

The Chelsea House Library of Biography
SENIOR EDITOR Kathy Kuhtz

Staff for **BARBARA BUSH**
COPY EDITOR Christopher Duffy
EDITORIAL ASSISTANT Tamar Levovitz
PICTURE RESEARCHER Melanie Sanford
DESIGNER Basia Niemczyc
COVER ILLUSTRATION Eileen McKeating

First Printing

1 3 5 7 9 8 6 4 2

Library of Congress Cataloging-in-Publication Data

Heiss, Arleen McGrath.
Barbara Bush/Arleen McGrath Heiss.
p. cm.—(The Chelsea House library of biography)
Includes bibliographical references and index.
Summary: A biography of the first lady, describing her formative years, her early married life, her role as a politician's and then a president's wife, and her volunteer work and activism.
ISBN 0-7910-1627-7
     0-7910-1634-X (pbk.)
1. Bush, Barbara, 1925– —Juvenile literature. 2. Bush, George, 1924– — Juvenile literature. 3. Presidents—United States—Wives—Biography—Juvenile literature. [1. Bush, Barbara, 1925– 2. First Ladies.] I. Title. II. Series.
E883.B87H45 1991   91-7829
973.928'092—dc20   CIP
[B]   AC

CONTENTS

THE CHELSEA HOUSE LIBRARY OF BIOGRAPHY

Other titles in the series are forthcoming.

Introduction

Learning from Biographies

Vito Perrone

The oldest narratives that exist are biographical. Much of what we know, for example, about the Pharaohs of ancient Egypt, the builders of Babylon, the philosophers of Greece, the rulers of Rome, the many biblical and religious leaders who provide the base for contemporary spiritual beliefs, has come to us through biographies—the stories of their lives. Although an oral tradition was long the mainstay of historically important biographical accounts, the oral stories making up this tradition became by the 1st century A.D. central elements of a growing written literature.

In the 1st century A.D., biography assumed a more formal quality through the work of such writers as Plutarch, who left us more than 500 biographies of political and intellectual leaders of Rome and Greece. This tradition of focusing on great personages lasted well into the 20th century and is seen as an important means of understanding the history of various times and places. We learn much, for example, from Plutarch's writing about the collapse of the Greek city-states and about the struggles in Rome over the justice and the constitutionality of a world empire. We also gain considerable understanding of the definitions of morality and civic virtue and how various common men and women lived out their daily existence.

Not surprisingly, the earliest American writing, beginning in the 17th century, was heavily biographical. Those Europeans who came to America were dedicated to recording their experience, especially the struggles they faced in building what they determined to be a new culture. John Norton's *Life and Death of John Cotton*, printed in 1630, typifies these early works. Later biographers often tackled more ambitious projects. Cotton Mather's *Magnalia Christi Americana*, published in 1702, accounted for the lives of more than 70 ministers and political leaders. In addition, a biographical literature around the theme of Indian captivity had considerable popularity. Soon after the American Revolution and the organization of the United States of America, Americans were treated to a large outpouring of biographies about such figures as Benjamin Franklin, George Washington, Thomas Jefferson, and Aaron Burr, among others. These particular works served to build a strong sense of national identity.

Among the diverse forms of historical literature, biographies have been over many centuries the most popular. And in recent years interest in biography has grown even greater, as biography has gone beyond prominent government figures, military leaders, giants of business, industry, literature, and the arts. Today we are treated increasingly to biographies of more common people who have inspired others by their particular acts of courage, by their positions on important social and political issues, or by their dedicated lives as teachers, town physicians, mothers, and fathers. Through this broader biographical literature, much of which is featured in the CHELSEA HOUSE LIBRARY OF BIOGRAPHY, our historical understandings can be enriched greatly.

What makes biography so compelling? Most important, biography is a human story. In this regard, it makes of history something personal, a narrative with which we can make an intimate connection. Biographers typically ask us as readers to accompany them on a journey through the life of another person, to see some part of the world through another's eyes. We can, as a result, come to understand what it is like to live the life of a slave, a farmer, a textile worker, an engineer, a poet, a president—in a sense, to walk in another's shoes. Such experience can be personally invaluable. We cannot ask for a better entry into historical studies.

Although our personal lives are likely not as full as those we are reading about, there will be in most biographical accounts many common experiences. As with the principal character of any biography, we are also faced with numerous decisions, large and small. In the midst of living our lives we are not usually able to comprehend easily the significance of our daily decisions or grasp easily their many possible consequences, but we can gain important insights into them by seeing the decisions made by others play themselves out. We can learn from others.

Because biography is a personal story, it is almost always full of surprises. So often, the personal lives of individuals we come across historically are out of view, their public personas masking who they are. It is through biography that we gain access to their private lives, to the acts that define who they are and what they truly care about. We see their struggles within the possibilities and limitations of life, gaining insight into their beliefs, the ways they survived hardships, what motivated them, and what discouraged them. In the process we can come to understand better our own struggles.

As you read this biography, try to place yourself within the subject's world. See the events as that person sees them. Try to understand why the individual made particular decisions and not others. Ask yourself if you would have chosen differently. What are the values or beliefs that guide the subject's actions? How are those values or beliefs similar to yours? How are they different from yours? Above all, remember: You are engaging in an important historical inquiry as you read a biography, but you are also reading a literature that raises important personal questions for you to consider.

*Barbara Bush and Raisa Gorbachev pose for pictures at the 1990
graduation ceremony at Wellesley College in Wellesley, Massachusetts. Both the controversy that surrounded the day and the
presence of Raisa Gorbachev turned the event into a media circus.*

1

Barbara Bush Speaks Out

JUNE 1, 1990, WAS A WARM, sunny day in Wellesley, Massachusetts. On a grassy lawn spread at the foot of a hill, next to a lake glinting in the sunshine, 575 women, seniors about to graduate from Wellesley College, sat beneath a large yellow-and-white-striped tent, excitedly awaiting their commencement speaker. Since the founding of the school in 1870, the scene had been repeated every year without much variation. But the cluster of television crews from ABC, CBS, NBC, CNN, and C-Span networks, radio transmitter trucks, and newspaper reporters at the side of the tent was far from traditional. Walkie-talkies crackled with static as dark-suited Secret Service men radioed terse instructions to one another, and a uniformed officer led a German shepherd trained to sniff for bombs around the tent and podium. Many relatives and friends of the graduates were forced to stand behind temporary crowd-control fences. Such features were not a usual part of the annual celebration. Finally, the cause of all this commotion stepped to the podium. As the camera crews swung into action, Barbara Bush, the wife of George Bush, president of the United States, began her commencement speech. Behind her sat Raisa Gorbachev, the wife of Mikhail Gorbachev, the leader of the Soviet Union.

Barbara Bush's presence as a public speaker was certainly not out of the ordinary. Even before her husband became president—while George had held the positions of vice-president, U.S. congressman from Texas, chairman of the Republican National party, and U.S. liaison to China—she had appeared at public functions many times. In fact, she had given a speech at Wellesley College more than 10 years before on her experiences in the People's Republic of China. She had been invited several months earlier to speak at the 1990 commencement. But a sour note was heard amid all of the excitement. One-quarter of the young women graduating that day had signed a petition protesting the selection of Barbara Bush as their commencement speaker. Three weeks before the petition's circulation, Barbara had invited Raisa Gorbachev to accompany her to Wellesley.

During her initial months as first lady, Barbara had spoken at school graduations, anniversary commemorations, fund-raisers, and conferences of all types. Within the first 100 days of the Bush administration, she had chosen to accept an invitation to speak at the commencement ceremony at Bennett College, a small black women's college in Greensboro, North Carolina, to great acclaim and appreciation. She was attracted to the college because of its commitment to literacy programs for young children and single mothers. One graduate's mother described her visit to the campus as "the best honor we could have." She added, "Nobody could have topped her, except maybe Oprah [Winfrey]." Visiting the school was one of Barbara's first official acts, and many praised her for reaching out to minorities. But rumbles of the dispute that divided the Wellesley campus had been heard in September 1989, when Barbara spoke at the convocation ceremony marking the beginning of the academic year at Smith

College in Massachusetts, another of the original Seven Sisters colleges. (The Seven Sisters are a group of colleges, originally founded for women, that are akin to the once all-male Ivy League.) At the convocation, Barbara accepted an honorary doctorate of humane letters for her volunteer work dedicated to literacy, the homeless, and the seriously ill, although she had dropped out of Smith after her freshman year 45 years earlier to marry George Bush. Smith shared in the Seven Sisters tradition of commitment to academic excellence, to educating women, and to volunteer service. Its student body, alumnae, and faculty were much like that of Wellesley's, and some of the objections raised by the Wellesley petition were voiced at Smith, although they received less media coverage. Some students at Smith felt it was inappropriate to honor a woman who did not have a career of her own and who did not publicly support women's rights, a cause in which many at the college fervently believed. Four seniors at convoca-

Susana Cárdenas (left) and Peggy Reid hold the flowers they will present to the first lady at the Wellesley commencement. Earlier, the two graduates had begun a petition drive that questioned Barbara's validity as a role model for young women of the 1990s.

tion wore T-shirts with a portrait of Nancy Reagan, the former first lady, captioned "Smith Class of 1943" next to a portrait of Barbara, captioned "Left in '44 to marry George." After spotting the shirts, Barbara told the wearers: "I don't like that shirt. Turn around." When they did, she read the message on the back: "There must be a better way to get a Smithy into the White House." Barbara laughed and commented, "You're absolutely right." She did not respond to students who carried a banner objecting to her personal silence on women's rights issues or others who objected to the college giving Barbara an honorary degree. For most observers, Barbara's personal political opinions were irrelevant to the visit, and the Smith crowd of 2,700 stomped and cheered Barbara's speech. Only a few news commentators drew attention to the event.

The petition at Wellesley caused much more controversy. A large part of the nation was deeply surprised that anyone would consider Barbara an inappropriate graduation speaker. She had successfully raised five children; aided her husband's political career; served as a volunteer for the March of Dimes, the Junior League, and many other service organizations; and founded a national campaign to

Barbara delivers her poignant yet humorous commencement address. The speech, well received by the audience, including the press, prompted TV anchor Tom Brokaw to call it "one of the best commencement speeches I've ever heard."

combat illiteracy. Much of the country respected her for her devotion to traditional values and ideals and loved her for her warm, down-to-earth personality and style. When Wellesley seniors Susana Cárdenas and Peggy Reid began their petition drive questioning Barbara's invitation, they unleashed a storm of debate and outrage in the nation's media. The core argument of their protest letter, signed by 150 seniors, was that Barbara was not invited because of her personal achievements. They believed that the story of her life had little in it to inspire young women of the 1990s. She had never had a career or worked outside the home. The petitioners felt that she had never grappled with the conflicting demands of work and family or developed a personal identity as a woman beyond that of an adjunct to a successful man. They felt she had been invited solely because she was married to the president.

The 150 students who challenged the value of having Barbara Bush speak at their commencement were stunned by the media's spirited defense of the first lady. The affair also raised questions about fundamental assumptions regarding options for modern women. Joan Ganz Cooney wrote in a *New York Times* op-ed article that both sides—critics and supporters—were misled by the American myth that women really can make a decision about entering the workplace or becoming a full-time homemaker. Cooney suggested that the students were probably upset because there is no longer a choice to do one or the other; like most men, most women have no choice—they must work for a living. Katha Pollitt wrote in the *Nation* that Cooney's line of thinking "hopelessly clouds the issue." To her, the controversy was not about the worth of raising children versus paid work. She felt the Wellesley invitation sent the graduates the "strange message" that "despite everything we've told you about defining yourself on your own terms, you ought to let a man do it for you and bask in reflected glory when his ship comes in." The discussion raged on. *Boston Globe* columnist Mike Barnicle called the students

Barbara and Raisa chat with Nannerl Keohane (center), president of Wellesley College. In her commencement speech, Keohane pointed out that although career options for a young woman in the 1940s were few, today she has "doors open to her which were closed to Mrs. Bush."

"unshaven feminists." Congresswoman Pat Schroeder of Colorado told *USA Today*, "Being a wife and mother isn't a protestable offense. After all, if it weren't for mothers, there would be no students at Wellesley." The original issue of whether status derived from marriage or recognition gained by individual achievement was more important to women was virtually lost in the barrage of articles about the controversy. Most of the writers grappled with the problem of whether supporting careers for women necessarily meant denigrating the value of full-time motherhood but ended with an affirmation of support for America's first lady.

Barbara was aware of the protest but never considered declining the invitation. She told a reporter from *U.S. News & World Report* that the protesters were "very reasonable. They're 21 years old, and they're looking at life from a different perspective. I don't disagree with what they're looking at. . . . In my day, they would have been considered different. In their day, I'm considered different. *Vive la différence*." She felt that she had something important to tell the seniors that day, something that she could share that would be relevant to their life. The students responded with warmth as Cárdenas and Reid presented Barbara with flowers and another group of students gave her a petition welcoming her to the college—and asking her to take a stronger public position on women's issues. As Barbara began her speech, after thanking Wellesley president Nannerl Keohane, the attendees, the class officers, and Mrs. Gorbachev, she announced, "I really am thrilled to be here today." Her blue eyes sparkled with genuine enthusiasm.

She opened with a brief anecdote from author Robert Fulghum's popular book *All I Really Need to Know I Learned in Kindergarten*. Quoting Fulghum's story about a young pastor who began a game of "Giants, Wizards, and Dwarves" to amuse some small children, she explained how the pastor told the children to decide which of the three—giant, wizard, or dwarf—they each wanted to be. A little girl asked, "But where do the mermaids stand?" Told that there are no mermaids, she replied, "Oh yes there are. I am a mermaid." Barbara pointed out that the little girl should not have to give up her identity to play the game or give up the game because of who she was. She urged the students to "respect difference, to be compassionate with one another, to cherish our own identity." She went on to list three important choices she felt the graduates should consider making. Urging them first to involve themselves with large issues, she mentioned her own commitment to literacy as a way of improving society. She noted that one should choose to have fun, that "life really must have joy. It's supposed to be fun!" Of her commitment to her husband, she said that "shared laughter has been one of our strongest bonds." Finally, she came to the core of her speech, what she thought she could share with the students: "The third choice that must not be missed is to cherish your human connections: Your relationships

with family and friends . . . those human connections—
with spouses, with children, with friends—are the most
important investments you will ever make." Applause
greeted her throughout the speech, and she closed with a
flash of humor, recognizing the changes that had taken
place for American women and anticipating more changes
ahead. To laughter and cheers, she announced: "And who
knows? Somewhere out in this audience may even be
someone who will one day follow in my footsteps, and
preside over the White House as the president's spouse,
and I wish him well!"

Raisa Gorbachev's short speech followed hers. Only a
few years before, relations between the United States and
the Soviet Union were unfriendly, a legacy of the decades-
long struggle between them known as the cold war. To see
the wife of the Soviet president speaking at a small college
graduation outside Boston was a stunning symbol of the
changes that had taken place in U.S.-Soviet relations after
Mikhail Gorbachev's ascendancy to power—changes due
to his vision and efforts. Barbara had scored a tremendous
public relations coup by bringing Raisa Gorbachev as her
guest. Raisa, speaking through an interpreter, acknowledged the enormous changes in the Soviet Union and the
world and recalled her own graduation from Moscow State
University years before. Referring to the need for international understanding, she ended with a plea for the
graduates to remember: "Your generation will soon as-
sume the responsibility for everything that takes place on
our planet." The audience gave her a resounding ovation.

Wellesley president Nannerl Keohane made it clear in
her speech that the questions raised by the "commencement controversy of 1990" were not about "disrespect
to the First Lady, which was never in the mind of any
Wellesley woman, nor underestimating the value of
motherhood and volunteering and nurturing, which we
profess as part of our college creed of service. Instead, the
questions are about whether society will allow young

women to become whole persons, expressing our talents and ambitions and dreams individually . . . defining ourselves, rather than being defined by stereotypes of gender or race or class." She pointed out: "The options for women have indeed become more diverse since the 1940s, when Barbara Pierce left Smith to marry George Bush and start a family. Today, a young woman in the Class of 1990 might make the same decision, for the same reasons. But she would also have doors open to her which were closed to Mrs. Bush and her classmates." Gracefully, she recognized both the value of the students' aspirations and the considerable achievements of Barbara Bush.

The graduates received their degrees, tossed their caps in the air, and marched jubilantly out of the tent. The day and the speeches had been a huge success, thanks in large part to Barbara Bush. Her appearance was covered live by all the television networks who had sent crews and was carried on Soviet, Japanese, and other foreign television networks. Her remarks were broadcast over the radio around the world. Commentators praised and quoted her speech in newspapers all over the country. NBC anchor Tom Brokaw called it "one of the best commencement speeches I've ever heard." Even though Barbara had given the same speech at several other schools that season, the surrounding circumstances and her heartfelt delivery made it touch the audience particularly deeply at Wellesley. As she and Raisa Gorbachev left the suburb of Wellesley, they stopped to visit schoolchildren at the public school there and at a school in nearby Boston, spreading goodwill and wishes for the future. Barbara Bush had helped turn what might have been a scene of bitterness, resentment, and controversy into a pleasant and rewarding experience for almost all concerned while firmly reasserting her values and beliefs. Those values had sustained her through 29 moves, 45 years of marriage, the death of a child, tough political campaigns, and all the pressures inherent in becoming and being the first lady of the United States.

Christine Bicknell, the 1990 student commencement speaker, confidently tells the Wellesley graduates that they will meet the challenges that the world holds in store for them.

Barbara Pierce, in a photo taken during her teen years, poses with her dog Sandy. Barbara has always loved dogs and has never been without one since childhood.

2

"The First Man I Ever Kissed"

BARBARA PIERCE, the third child of Marvin and Pauline Pierce, was born on June 8, 1925, in New York City, and soon her parents brought her home from the hospital to join her older siblings Martha and James in the family home in Rye, New York. Martha was five years old; James was three years old. Barbara remained the baby of the family until the arrival of her brother Scott five years later.

Marvin Pierce, 31 years old when Barbara was born, had chosen for his family a five-bedroom brick house on a quarter-acre lot in Rye, a fashionable town of 8,000 in Westchester County on Long Island Sound. He was from a family whose ancestry included Franklin Pierce, the president of United States from 1853 to 1857, who was his great-great-uncle. The Pierce family's wealth came from their Ohio iron foundry business, but their financial situation had changed dramatically in 1893, when the price of iron plummeted. By the time Marvin Pierce, born in 1893, reached college age, the family fortune still had not recovered, and he had to postpone his entrance to college for two years in order to help out his family financially. He worked as a surveyor and as a teaching assistant before starting school at Miami University in Oxford, Ohio.

Marvin's achievements in college were outstanding both in the classroom and on the playing field. He was a tennis star, captain of the football team, and pitcher on the baseball team and graduated with high academic honors. Later, he earned advanced degrees in engineering from the Massachusetts Institute of Technology and Harvard College in Cambridge, Massachusetts. While at Miami University, he met Pauline Robinson. She was a well-known campus beauty who was attending neighboring Oxford

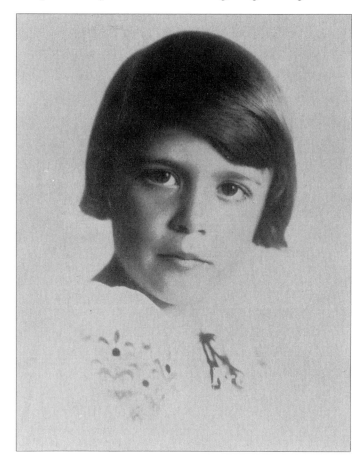

Barbara, the third child of Pauline and Marvin Pierce, was born in New York City on June 8, 1925.

College and was the daughter of an Ohio Supreme Court judge. The two fell in love and were married in 1918.

After serving in World War I, Pierce went to work in New York City as a clerk in the McCall corporation, a publishing company that produced *Redbook* and *McCall's* magazines (two popular women's periodicals) and the immensely popular McCall's sewing pattern catalogs. About one year after the family moved from New York City to Rye, he was promoted to vice-president of the firm. In 1934 he became a director and in 1946 was voted president of *McCall's*. His success provided the family with a comfortable way of life.

The small town of Rye was a suburb of New York City, and every day, men boarded trains for the daily commute to and from jobs in Manhattan. Meanwhile, their wives stayed at home to look after the children and to provide volunteer service for the social and civic well-being of the town. Many of Rye's families were financially secure, if not wealthy, and the wives did not need to work. The Pierces were no exception.

Barbara's mother, Pauline, had the time and resources to pursue many interests, or "enthusiasms," as her children later called them: gardening, antique collecting, and needlepoint. She was as unathletic as her husband was athletic. Instead of playing tennis or golf, she devoted her time to volunteer activities and clubs. Barbara later referred to her mother as a "joiner."

The Pierce family enjoyed what Barbara described as a life surrounded by "luxury," enjoying a beautiful home, household help, private schools, and clubs. Yet Pauline tended to be "undisciplined" about money, as Barbara remembered. In an interview in later years Barbara recalled that if her mother got $10 she would spend $20 and never hesitated to say "charge it" if she wanted to buy something. Marvin Pierce's job ensured that the family never suffered from the effects of the Great Depression of the 1930s, but his wife's spending occasionally caused him concern.

The Pierces, however, did endure troubled times that had nothing to do with finances. Their youngest child, Scott, developed a cyst on his shoulder bone when he was two years old, and Pauline, whom Barbara described as a "very good mother," devoted an enormous amount of her time to his care. For seven years Pauline herself commuted to Manhattan, taking Scott to New York hospitals for bone grafts and other surgery. The strain of his illness was felt throughout the family, but they pulled together. Marvin Pierce had a wonderful sense of humor, which eased the tension. Barbara's sensibility was much like her father's, and she felt particularly close to him. In several interviews Barbara has indicated she was closer to her father than her mother. She, Martha, James, and Scott enjoyed his teasing, although Pauline, who was often the target of family ribbing and lacked a good sense of humor, sometimes did not.

Both parents taught important values to their children. According to Donnie Radcliffe's 1989 book, *Simply Barbara Bush*, Barbara described how "the world was more beautiful" because of her mother. Her mother was not perfect but taught the family "a lot of good lessons." Her father wanted to give his children "a fine education, a good example, and all the love in the world." Accordingly, they were taught to "look after people's feelings" and were brought up with a sense of responsibility to their community and to people in need. The Pierce children also grew up with their parents' deep love for reading books. Barbara described an early memory of her father and mother reading by the fireplace and all the children "curled up with something." As a child, Barbara walked to the Rye Public Library every Saturday to get books to read for the entire week. Her favorites included mysteries by Agatha Christie, novels by the Canadian writer Mazo de la Roche, and short stories published in the *Saturday Evening Post*.

Barbara, also called Bar, attended the public Milton School (seen here in a 1947 photograph) in Rye, New York, until the seventh grade, when she transferred to the private Rye Country Day School.

Barbara grew up to value her parents' lessons and devotion to reading.

Barbara's formal education began in the fall of 1931 at Rye's public Milton School. Barbara remembers being brought to the classroom by her mother, who then left quietly without saying good-bye. At first, six-year-old Barbara felt abandoned, but she found she loved school so much that by the time she got home, she had forgiven her mother. She attended Milton until the seventh grade, when she transferred to the private Rye Country Day School.

Radcliffe elicited many memories from Barbara about her childhood. Barbara, also called "Bar," was a "popular, fun-loving, and outgoing youngster" who idolized her sister, Martha, was "scared to death of her brother James," and adored her brother Scott, whom she remembered as "uncomplaining and unspoiled." Barbara and Scott often walked their father to the train station in the morning, before boarding the school bus. She recalled that James tended to get in trouble, and she gleefully took on the role of a "merciless tease who could hardly wait to expose James's misdeeds." She was in awe of her sister, who was extremely attractive.

Barbara (far left) portrays the role of Beatrice in a 1942 production of William Shakespeare's Much Ado About Nothing. *Drama and sports were just two of the many school activities in which Barbara participated while attending Ashley Hall in Charleston, South Carolina.*

Barbara followed in the footsteps of her sister Martha and left Rye at the beginning of her junior year of high school to attend a small, exclusive girls' preparatory school in Charleston, South Carolina, called Ashley Hall. Barbara remembered it as a world of its own, bounded by strict rules about good manners and proper behavior. The 150 students from around the country were not allowed to wear makeup or to have steady boyfriends. In fact, the school forbade its students to date the same man on consecutive weekends. A student could be deemed "bad" if she were caught leaving the school grounds without hat, stockings, and gloves.

Barbara described herself as "desolate" when she began the overnight train trip to Charleston. Once at school, she was miserable "for about four minutes," until she met some other students. Her time quickly filled with studies, school plays, sports, and dates in the parlor on Sunday afternoons. Known for her fun-loving nature, Barbara's mischievous activities included "eating the most hot, buttered biscuits in one meal without getting caught." But the charming atmosphere of the school was shattered on December 7, 1941, by the news that the Japanese had bombed Pearl Harbor, a U.S. naval base in Hawaii. The nation entered World War II and joined Great Britain, France, and later the Soviet Union in fighting the Axis powers: Japan in the Pacific and Germany and Italy in Europe.

Despite the war, Christmas festivities went on. While home on Christmas break from Ashley Hall, Barbara attended a "Get Together" party at the Round Hill Country Club in nearby Greenwich, Connecticut. She described the evening to Donnie Radcliffe many years later. At the age of 16, Barbara was 5 feet 8 inches tall. She was a slender girl, with blue eyes and reddish brown hair. She chose to wear an off-the-shoulder dress in red and green, in keeping with the holiday spirit.

Barbara, whom one of her friends described as a "vision" that night, caught the eye of what she remembers as "the handsomest boy I had ever seen." A 17-year-old

While home from boarding school one summer, Barbara (left) and two friends, Rosanne "Posy" Morgan (center) and Kate Siedle, make believe they are statues in an empty fountain. Barbara fondly remembers her years growing up in Rye; she is said to have inherited her father's wonderful sense of humor.

George Herbert Walker Bush (first row, center), captain of the baseball team, poses with his teammates at Phillips Academy in Andover, Massachusetts. George, an outstanding student and athlete, was a senior when he met Barbara at a Christmas dance in Greenwich, Connecticut, in 1941.

senior at Phillips Academy in Andover, Massachusetts, George Herbert Walker Bush (nicknamed Poppy) was spending Christmas break at home with his family in Greenwich. An outstanding student and athlete, the young man was the head of many clubs, teams, and associations at his prestigious, academically rigorous school. After a mutual friend introduced the two teens, Poppy asked Barbara to dance. Described as a "generic" dancer who usually did the fox-trot to everything, Poppy was at a loss when the band played a waltz, and he asked Barbara to sit and talk until the piece ended. They sat and talked for the rest of the evening. Barbara did not seem to notice his lack of dancing ability; she later told Radcliffe, "I could hardly breathe when he was in the room."

Barbara also told Radcliffe about the next night, when Poppy and Barbara both attended a dance at the Apawamis Club in Rye. Her excitement at seeing the attractive Phil-

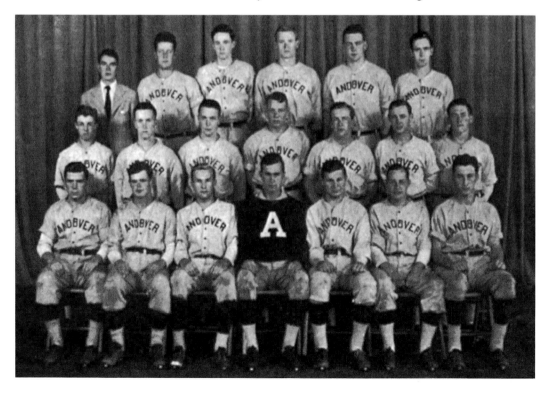

lips student quickly turned to fury at her brother James when, ignoring Barbara, he cut in on their dance to ask Poppy to play in an upcoming YMCA basketball game. But Barbara made sure she was at the contest, and Poppy arranged to borrow one of the family cars to drive her home after the game, which her whole family attended. Worried about long, awkward silences between him and his date, Poppy asked his father to let him use the big family car with the radio. His trepidation proved unfounded, for he later teased that Barbara "started talking that night and hasn't stopped since."

Both George (his childhood nickname did not stick long) and Barbara returned to school after the holidays. Nothing in their life was quite as it had been before the Christmas break. The escalating war continued to pull young men away from home. George was planning to enlist in the U.S. Navy as soon as he graduated. He wrote to Barbara frequently. Despite the distance between South Carolina and Massachusetts, their relationship grew stronger. After graduating from high school, George went ahead with his plan and joined the navy on June 12, 1942, his 18th birthday. He became a seaman, second class, and was assigned to preflight training in Chapel Hill, North Carolina. There, as at Phillips, he excelled. When he was awarded his wings upon completion of his training as a pilot, he became the youngest aviator in U.S. naval history.

In June 1943, Barbara graduated from Ashley Hall. At George's invitation, in August she visited the Bush family summer home in Kennebunkport, Maine, where the Bushes have vacationed since 1902. Barbara thoroughly enjoyed spending time with George and getting to know his parents, Dorothy and Prescott Bush, and his siblings, before George had to report back to duty for advanced flight training. The specter of his upcoming departure and participation in combat shadowed their time together.

In his autobiography, George described how the pressures of the war affected young people at the time. The

Barbara and George relax with Bucky, George's youngest brother. In August 1943, Barbara was invited to vacation at the Bushes' summer home in Kennebunkport, Maine.

stresses they felt gave them what psychologists later described as "heightened awareness"—an overwhelming uncertainty about the future and an increased appreciation of the present. Young couples tended to become "serious" very quickly, and at the time, visits to each other's families were considered a clear indication of a growing commitment. By the end of her visit that August, Barbara and George were secretly engaged—they thought. As George reported in *Looking Forward*, it was "secret, to the extent that the German and Japanese high commands weren't aware of it." Everyone else had taken for granted that George and Barbara were headed for the altar. Family and friends could see that they were in love, even though the couple had not seen each other often during their 18-month courtship. Neither George nor Barbara will discuss any details of their courtship. Barbara cannot describe how or where George proposed because she claims he never actually did. Somehow it was decided. Their engagement was announced in the *New York Times* in December.

World War II raged on in Europe and in the Pacific Ocean. As George's torpedo squadron headed for active duty in the Pacific, Barbara entered prestigious Smith College in Northampton, Massachusetts, in September 1943. Social life at the exclusive Seven Sisters school was severely curtailed, for the number of men at neighboring colleges was few—most of them were at war. Barbara did make lots of friends at Smith, became captain of the freshman soccer team, and admitted that she "preferred to think about George Bush, off in the South Pacific," rather than study. Following the reports of troop movements and battles could be very absorbing, and reading the casualty lists in the newspapers could be extremely sobering. Barbara found "she was just interested in George." At the beginning of her sophomore year she took a leave of absence from college and returned home.

George became a member of the VT-51 squadron and the pilot of a Grumman Avenger plane, which he nicknamed Barbara. During the fall of 1944, he was the aviator in a three-man crew that also included a turret gunner and a radioman–tail gunner. The plane carried a 2,000-pound payload of bombs for use in torpedo runs, antisubmarine patrols, glide bombings, and cover for amphibious landings (landings of ground forces from ships). Although considered the biggest and best single-engine bomber, the sturdy Avenger was not the fastest. The plane was known to be "low and slow."

On September 2, 1944, George and his crew, which included William White, whose father had been a classmate of Prescott Bush's at Yale, flew over Chichi Jima in a raid that targeted a Japanese radio communications cen-

Freshman Barbara Pierce reads a book on some steps at Smith College. In the fall of 1944—during World War II—she decided to discontinue her college studies and withdrew from Smith.

During World War II, George sits in the cockpit of his navy Grumman Avenger plane, which he nicknamed Barbara. While Barbara anxiously waited at home for his return, George flew 58 combat missions and received the Distinguished Flying Cross for an air raid on Chichi Jima, Japan.

ter on the Bonin Islands, only 600 miles from Tokyo. The Japanese fiercely defended the islands, and George's Avenger was shot down. George was able to parachute to safety in the open sea, but the other crew members were lost. George clung to a life raft—what had been his seat cushion on the Avenger—until he was rescued by an American submarine. Eight weeks later he finally was able to leave the sub and return to his squadron. During the two months George spent on the sub, no one told Barbara her fiancé had been shot down, and years later she claimed she was grateful for the deception. By December 1944, the VT-51 squadron was rotated out of combat, and George was ordered home on leave after completing 58 combat missions. He received the Distinguished Flying Cross for the raid on Chichi Jima and three other air medals.

George and Barbara wanted to get married as soon as possible. In *Flight of the Avenger: George Bush at War*, Joe Hyams quotes part of a letter George sent his brother Jonathan that reveals George's impatience and gleeful expectations. George commanded, "Whip out your top hat and tails, cause I want you to be one of the featured ushers at my wedding—when it will be I do not know, but get hot on shining your shoes, cause the day is not far off. Also get pants that are plenty big, because we're going to fill you so full of champagne it'll be coming out of your ears." Although Barbara and George had planned a wedding on December 19, George did not arrive home until Christmas Eve. So 19-year-old Barbara Pierce and 20-year-old George Herbert Walker Bush were married on January 6, 1945, at the First Presbyterian Church in Rye. Barbara wore a long-sleeved, appliquéd white satin gown and Dorothy Bush's wedding veil. George wore dress navy blues. Almost 300 people attended the reception at the Apawamis Club in Rye. Barbara recalled that the guests were "mostly women and old folks" because of the continuing war.

The newlyweds honeymooned at The Cloisters, a hotel on Sea Island, Georgia. In *George Bush: An Intimate Portrait*, author Fitzhugh Green reports that Nancy Bush Ellis, George's sister, received a letter from him while he was still on Sea Island. He wrote with enthusiasm: "Married life exceeds all expectations. Barbara is a fine wife!" For her part, Barbara called her marriage the "biggest turning point in my life." She is often quoted as saying, "I married the first man I ever kissed." She has also wryly noted that she made a wise choice for the long run, for the beau she was seeing when she met George was trying marriage for the fourth time by the time George Bush became vice-president of the United States.

After the honeymoon, George was still on active duty in the navy. Together George and Barbara made their first home in a one-room basement apartment in Wyandotte, Michigan, not far from the Grosse Ile Naval Air Station. Barbara faced her new responsiblity—homemaking— with little guidance or experience. The Pierce family had never been without household help, and Barbara's mother did not offer her daughter much advice. Pauline Pierce had a theory that if you could read, you could learn to run a house. Barbara had to learn by trial and error. In *Running Mates*, Ann Grimes tells the story of how Barbara's first errors were sometimes costly. In one apartment where the Bushes stayed, the landlady showed Barbara how to run the washing machine. Barbara promptly filled it with all the handmade silk lingerie she had received as part of her trousseau—and ruined every piece in the load.

After their stay in Michigan, the Bushes moved to posts in Maine and Virginia. In August 1945, World War II ended, and the United States rejoiced. George was happy that he could return to civilian life and resume his education. He and Barbara moved to New Haven, Connecticut, and George enrolled in Yale University, his father's alma mater. After Barbara took her leave of absence from Smith, she never returned. She could not attend Yale with George because at the time it was an all-male institution. In fact, she never did complete her college education. Years later, she has occasionally expressed regrets about her lack of a college degree. In truth, she simply did not want to go back. The vast majority of women of her generation did not complete their education, and for those who did, meaningful, challenging, well-paying jobs were practically nonexistent. Instead of going back to school, Barbara settled in with George at Yale, worked at the Yale Co-op, a bookstore, and helped George with his volunteer work for the United Negro College Fund.

On July 6, 1946, George Walker Bush was born. (Although he is not technically a "junior," the Bushes sometimes refer to him that way.) The family lived off campus, in an old house that had been divided into 13 small apartments. Each of the 13 students who lived in the building was a veteran and each was married. By the time little George was born, the 13 couples had already produced 14 children. The postwar baby boom was under way.

War veterans were more anxious to earn their degrees and move on to good jobs than prewar students had been. They tended to work hard and complete their education faster, for the war had delayed the progress of their life. George, who majored in economics, graduated with honors and received a Phi Beta Kappa key, an emblem of membership in the select society for academic excellence, after only two and a half years at Yale. A star athlete on the varsity baseball team, he played first base on a team that produced a major-leaguer, Frank Quinn. He was also inducted into the secret and highly selective Skull and Bones society, as his father and his father's business partner, William Averell Harriman, had been. (In the 1940s, Harriman was the U.S. ambassador to the USSR, then later became secretary of the U.S. Department of Commerce, and in 1954 was elected governor of New York.) Under George's name the 1948 Yale yearbook lists 25 activities

and achievements that occupied his short time at the university. Green noted that Barbara must have been a good partner, because she gave George the "mental and emotional equilibrium to accomplish all that he did."

A world of options were available to George after graduation. He had an offer from his father's investment firm, despite its rule against hiring the relatives of employees. His academic achievement had attracted a number of big companies looking for management trainees. He and Barbara even briefly considered farming. Ultimately he was attracted to the Southwest, where businesses of all types were racing to meet the demands of the booming postwar economy. George was anxious to get into what he called the "real world." He saw great opportunity in the growing petroleum industry, and the family of three was soon on its way to a establish a new life on its own.

Barbara and George, as a young married couple, pose for a photograph. After their wedding, on January 6, 1945, and honeymoon, Barbara and George moved to Michigan, where George was sent by the navy to serve at Grosse Ile Naval Air Station.

Texas oil gushes 700 feet into the air. In 1948, taking advantage of the great opportunities available in the petroleum industry, George joined the International Derrick and Equipment Company (Ideco) in Odessa, Texas.

3

Building the Foundations

GEORGE DROVE AWAY in his 1947 red Studebaker, a gift from his father, leaving Barbara and his young son temporarily behind. He saw a chance to make their fortune in hot, barren west Texas. Neil Mallon, a close friend of his father's who had attended Yale and joined the Skull and Bones society with him, suggested that the oil fields of Texas were "the place for amibitious young people these days." In 1948, the United States needed more and more oil to fuel its postwar manufacturing boom. The nation's factories turned from producing war matériel to producing peacetime consumer products such as automobiles, and the increasing number of cars meant even more demand for oil. George had seen some of Texas during his advanced flight training during the war, but he had never been to Odessa, where he was to join a subsidiary of Dresser Industries—the International Derrick and Equipment Company (Ideco)—as a trainee and clerk. As he continued his lonesome drive, he journeyed farther into the arid, desolate, almost treeless country and farther away from the country clubs, commuter trains, and manicured lawns of his and Barbara's youth.

Odessa was a shock to him. The rough little town was filled with almost nothing but oil-drilling equipment. Its cultural life centered around two small movie theaters that mainly showed westerns. He thought about his grandfather, James Smith Bush, who had left his comfortable life as a storekeeper to seek his fortune in the California Gold Rush, and how similar his own decision to leave the East had been.

George understood the challenges he faced. In addition to hard work and luck, he needed Barbara's understanding and support to face life in west Texas. One week after he arrived in Odessa, he sent for Barbara and their son to join him in their new home. It was difficult for Barbara to leave New England for Texas. Her friends and family would be half a nation away. She would lose the close contact she had with her mother, sister Martha, and Dorothy Bush, the mother-in-law she had come to adore.

Years later, in an interview with Michael Kilian, she spoke about how she had been brought up to believe that "if your husband wanted to do something, you'd do it gladly." She maintained that "there's nothing really wrong with that. I would say the same if a wife wanted to do something very badly. Her husband should do the same." The value she placed on loyalty to her spouse was shared by the majority of American women after the war. After years of deferring normal life and waiting for their men to return from the war, women seized their long-awaited opportunity to begin their own family life.

Within a week of sending for his wife and son, George located housing. With mixed emotions, Barbara headed off to Texas to become part of the world of oil wells, tumbleweeds, and chicken-fried steak. There was little housing in Odessa after the war, and what living space could be found was very different from that found in the East. Odessa's residents could not be too fussy about where they lived. Their choices included converted chicken coops, trailers, or apartments in a "shotgun shack." ("Shotgun shack" is slang for a long, narrow, usually dilapidated building consisting of one room after another in a straight line. Supposedly, a shotgun shell fired in the doorway would go directly through the entire house and out the back.)

A tiny apartment in a modified shotgun shack on unpaved East Seventh Street was where the Bush family settled. They had one bedroom with three beds, a small kitchen, and another room furnished with a table and three chairs. Two women and a child who lived in an apartment on the other side of a makeshift partition shared the bathroom with the Bushes. The Bushes did not have much

The Bushes' home in Odessa looked very much like this tiny shotgun shack. Barbara, who always tried to make the best of a bad situation, later commented on the unattractive structure, "As we had the only bathroom on the street, we didn't complain."

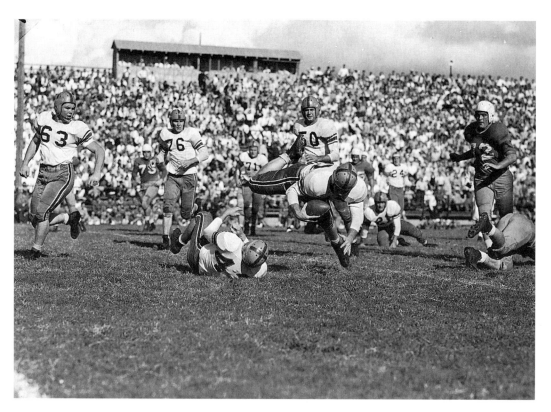

The football teams of Texas and Baylor Universities play a game in Waco in the late 1940s. Living in Odessa gave George and Barbara the opportunity to become caught up in the fever of the immensely popular sport of football.

in common with their neighbors. The sound of an ancient air conditioner in the connecting window could not conceal the noise made by the nightly stream of male visitors to the two women, who were prostitutes. Life in Texas was going to be very different from life in Westchester County.

Barbara, a self-proclaimed nester who loves to make her home a cozy refuge, had never dreamed of living in such conditions. But as she later explained: "Everything is relative in life. As we had the only bathroom on the street, we didn't complain." She understood the need to live and let live in her new home.

The young couple cheerfully settled into their new surroundings with more curiosity than complaints, but Pauline Pierce, Barbara's mother, had her own notions about Odessa. She kept sending them boxes of laundry soap because she was not convinced that they could buy such a thing in the wilds of Texas. Barbara had to reassure her mother that, yes, such necessities were available in stores. Contrary to its popular image in movies and novels, Texas was not a raw frontier. For the Bushes, it was a place to make new friends, raise a growing family, and discover an exciting new industry, Texas-style football fever, and the twang of Lone Star accents. Most of all, Texas gave them a chance to be independent.

Barbara enjoyed being on her own. Ann Grimes notes that Barbara told a *Los Angeles Times* interviewer that she had felt a bit overpowered by her mother, mother-in-law, and sister, who were all strong women. She admitted to the interviewer that when she lived at home, "my mother and sister bought everything and told me, 'This would be nice for you.'" Explaining that she considered the early move far from home to have been good for her marriage, she said, "When you are a couple all grown up, nobody's son or daughter, nobody's shadow, you are you." Supported by George's trainee salary of $300 a month, the little family felt they were doing just fine. Barbara noted in the *Times* interview: "George and I never thought we were poor. We knew if something terrible happened to us, we had family."

While Barbara worked hard to make the little apartment a home, George applied himself to learning about the oil industry—the different types of drill pipe and tubing, drilling masts, derricks, and all the other equipment and machinery used to extract oil from the ground. Before the year was over, George was transferred from Ideco in Odessa to another Dresser Industries subsidiary called Pacific Pumps, located in Huntington Park, California. In mid-1949, the company next sent him to Bakersfield, California, where he was promoted to the job of salesman. His new position required him to travel nearly 1,000 miles a week. Barbara found that her husband's demanding work schedule left her on her own more than ever before. During the period when George was a salesman on the road, Barbara and little George dealt with moves to Whittier,

Oil-field workers change drill bits on an oil well outside Snyder, Texas. George's job, selling drilling equipment, required him to travel frequently and forced him to leave Barbara alone for long periods of time. Barbara and George W. moved from town to town to be with him between trips.

Ventura, and Compton, California, in order to be with George between trips. While George and Barbara had been engaged, George had promised Barbara that if she would "stick with me, I'll show you the world." She certainly was seeing the country at least, town by town.

Early on, Barbara had developed the view that "life has its bumps" and "we should enjoy ourselves during the good times and make the most of the bad times." Unlike her mother, who, Barbara told Radcliffe, "always thought the grass was going to be greener sometime, some other place," Barbara decided that "life is right now." She often asserts that her life has always been happy, but early in her marriage, she had to contend with sadness as well.

In Compton, Barbara, at 24, became pregnant with their second child. Late in the pregnancy, during October 1949, she received horrifying news from New York. On a short drive to the train station in Rye, her parents were involved in an auto accident. Her father, seeing that a cup of hot coffee was about to spill on his wife, made a sudden move. He lost control of the car, which veered wildly and slammed into a stone wall. Marvin Pierce suffered broken ribs and facial bruises. Pauline Pierce was killed instantly.

The dreadful news was especially stressful for Barbara, 7 months pregnant and 3,000 miles away. Marvin Pierce, concerned about his daughter's condition, urged her not to undertake the long trip back to New York for the funeral and convinced Barbara not to leave Compton. Years later, she regretted the decision not to attend her mother's funeral. It was very difficult for her to be far from family during a tragedy, no matter how independent she was.

In December 1949, two months after her mother's death, Barbara gave birth to her second child. Because of the Bushes' many moves, Barbara did not even have a chance to meet the doctor until the day before the baby was born. Until decades later, men had no place in the delivery room and were actually barred from being present at the birth of their children. George maintained a vigil in the waiting room, as he had done for the birth of his son. Finally, he received the happy news that he and Barbara were the parents of a beautiful daughter. They decided to name the hazel-eyed, blond-haired infant Pauline Robinson Bush, after Barbara's mother. Soon she was nicknamed Robin.

The new year brought yet another move for the family of four. In 1950, George's job took him back to Texas, to Midland, a small town about 20 miles northeast of Odessa. The oil industry was booming, and oil company employees and independent speculators from all over the nation flooded into Midland and towns like it. Office space and housing were in high demand, but the Bushes found a

Barbara, George, and George W. stand in front of a Dresser Industries airplane with George's mother, Dorothy, and father, Prescott, who served as one of Dresser's directors until he was elected U.S. senator in 1952.

house of their own for $7,500 in a neighborhood called Easter Egg Row. The row was a subdivision—a block of land bought by a developer who divided the land into plots and constructed homes on them. Such subdivisions spread all over America in the 1950s as investors and developers took advantage of the exploding postwar baby boom and consequent need for housing. The builder of Easter Egg Row had erected all the houses in the development using the same floor plan, which included only 875 square feet of living space. None had a dining room. In fact, the only way to tell the neat, identical little houses apart was by the color of their paint and their location on the lot. Like thousands of other young families in the 1950s, the Bushes settled into their house, which was light blue, and proceeded to make their backyard the focal point of their social life. There were not many other places to socialize in the brand-new area.

Every day, the men of Midland went off to work, pursuing their dreams of oil wealth. The women stayed home— for several reasons. Throughout the 1950s, more than two-thirds of all married women were full-time housewives. Because housing prices and the cost of living were low then compared to later in the 20th century, one income could support a family, so that women did not need to work. American society and culture at the time actively discouraged women from working—help-wanted advertisements were segregated by sex, companies could legally refuse to hire women, and few women had college degrees. They raised their children, took care of the house, and spent their time supporting and building the community. In Midland, Barbara joined her fellow housewives in their efforts to build a local symphony orchestra and a theater.

Many young families from all over the country had come to live in Midland. Barbara and George grew particularly close to their new neighbors, and the group of friends treated each other like members of an extended family. They attended church and barbecues together, the men set up touch football games, and the women took turns watching each other's children. Most families in the area had four or more children. Barbara explained: "No one had any family nearby. We were all newcomers and came from all over the country. We formed really good friendships."

One friendship led to the creation of the Bush-Overby Oil Development Company, Inc. Late in 1950, George left Dresser Industries when he and John Overby, a neighbor, "caught the fever" to start an independent oil company. They took some of their savings, added it to money invested by Bush's family, and buckled down to the hard work of creating and running a business. Barbara's life revolved around raising her children and volunteering in Midland, which included working for the improvement of the performing arts, schools, and hospitals.

Except for a summer job at a hardware firm during World War II and her part-time work at the Yale Co-op, Barbara had never held a paying job. But her days were filled with activity, and she was well known for her open-door policy. She welcomed neighbors' children into her home and treated them like her own. She considered her role to be that of a "traditional, supportive mother." Her friends recall that she was a highly organized homemaker and a very good cook. One humorously remarked on Barbara's prowess, "She always made me feel like a slob." George praised her for always going "the extra mile." He noted she was always there for their children for "every inning of their Little League game or every tear to be wiped away, every broken heart later on in some young romance."

In a 1985 speech at American University in Washington, D.C., Barbara described the period as one of "long days and short years [filled with] diapers, runny noses, earaches, more Little League games than you could believe possible, tonsils . . . unscheduled races to the hospital emergency room, Sunday School and church, of hours of urging homework, or short chubby arms around your neck and sticky kisses." While George was hard at work traveling and expanding his business, Barbara managed the home. His life was never routine. He traveled more than ever before, but he was his own boss—a pioneer in search of both national and international business. His itinerary included North Dakota, New York City, London, The Hague, Mexico, and Trinidad; hers included the doctor's office, parent-teacher conferences, birthday parties, and baseball games. Wryly, she told an interviewer that she recalled thinking, "Well, George is off on a trip doing all these exciting things and I'm sitting home with these absolutely brilliant children, who say one thing a week of interest."

In later years she admitted that she had had a few "bumpy moments . . . feeling that I'd never, ever be able to have fun again; and coping with the feeling that George Bush, in his excitement of starting a small company and traveling around the world, was having a lot of fun." Her commitment to the importance of family stability made her willing to pay the price of raising her children primarily by herself without resentment.

Despite the bumpy moments during what Barbara termed her "dormant years," she was "perfectly happy to have children." On February 11, 1953, she gave birth to their third child, John Ellis Bush, called Jeb. But great sorrow intruded on these years. Radcliffe reports what Barbara told her about the following events.

While taking care of her brood one morning, Barbara was alarmed by Robin's sudden lack of interest in playing. Robin did not seem ill, but it was not like the rambunctious three-year-old to be so quiet. Concerned about Robin, Barbara took her to the pediatrician's office to see Dr. Dorothy Wyvell, a family friend as well as the children's physician. Unlike previous visits, Barbara did not hear the usual reassuring diagnosis of a little flu. The doctor took a blood sample and told Barbara to return in the afternoon for the results of a blood test. It was the kind of uncertainty all parents dread. After Barbara called George, he drove 20 miles back to town to be with her when the test results came in.

Dr. Wyvell informed the Bushes that Robin had the highest white blood cell count she had ever seen. Robin was suffering from terminal leukemia, a type of blood cancer. The Bushes were stunned; they had never heard of the disease. The doctor's advice was even more startling to the devastated couple. She told them: "Number one, don't tell anyone. Number two, don't treat her. You should take her home, make life as easy as possible for her, and in three weeks' time, she'll be gone."

In a 1988 interview, Barbara admitted the doctor had given "us the best advice anyone could have given, which of course we didn't take." Instead, the Bushes told their neighbors about Robin's condition, and the close-knit group responded with an outpouring of care and support. The next day, the Bushes flew with Robin to a New York City hospital, today's Memorial Sloan-Kettering Cancer Center, on the advice of George's uncle, Dr. John Walker, who was a cancer specialist and president of the New York Memorial Hospital. He urged them to treat Robin with all the resources of modern medicine.

Robin spent the next seven months struggling against the disease. Barbara never left her side, whether in the hospital in New York or at home in Midland. On weekends that Robin spent at Sloan-Kettering, George flew to Manhattan to be with her. At first the Bushes' neighbors took care of seven-year-old George and Jeb, who was still an infant. George's mother soon sent a nurse to Texas to care for her grandsons. The members of the Midland church that the Bushes attended and all their friends rallied around and tried to help in any way they could. Some sent food or cooked meals for the exhausted family; others even donated the blood Robin needed for her frequent transfusions.

Barbara did not want Robin to know how desperate her situation really was. She felt her daughter was too young to understand what was happening to her, and she spent all her time with Robin. At her insistence, no one was allowed to cry in Robin's room. However, both George and his mother, Dorothy, had difficulty observing the rule. Barbara tried to remain upbeat for her daughter's sake. During visits to Sloan-Kettering, Barbara became acquainted with the staff, the other patients, and the patients' families.

In October 1953, Robin had a serious hemorrhage, and her death was apparently very near. Barbara, only 28 years old, remained strong throughout the final hours. Doctors operated on Robin in a futile attempt to overcome the disease's final assault, but Robin did not survive the procedure. Both parents were with her when she died. The following day, George returned to the hospital to thank the staff for all they had done for his daughter. Many were crying, for they had become very close to Barbara and felt for her in her loss.

When Robin succumbed to leukemia at last, Barbara's courage deserted her. She told Radcliffe, "I just fell apart when Robin died. I hadn't cried at all when she was alive, but after she died I felt I could cry forever." Some of Barbara's friends believe that her hair turned completely white while she was in her thirties as a result of the tragedy. Barbara recalled that during the period following Robin's death, she could barely put one foot in front of the other. George stayed by her side and would not allow her to

In 1953, Robin, the Bushes' first daughter, died of leukemia at the age of three. Throughout the seven months that Robin fought the disease, the family drew much-needed support from one another and from friends.

Two volunteers assist physically challenged children at a March of Dimes facility during the 1950s. To overcome the heartache she suffered following Robin's death, Barbara threw herself into volunteer work with the March of Dimes and other organizations.

remain lost in her grief. He fought to bring her back to their two little boys.

Barbara recounted how George "held me in his arms, and made me share it, and accept that his sorrow was as great as my own. He simply wouldn't allow my grief to divide us . . . [or] push us apart." The strength of their commitment to each other and to their family helped them through one of the most difficult times a parent can face. As Barbara noted, as many as 70 percent of couples who experience the death of a child later divorce. Such partners tend to stop talking to one another and become isolated and unreachable in their separate grief. George's sensitivity and support and Barbara's relationship with him helped the Bushes stay close and remain together.

After Robin's death, the two boys became the center of Barbara's attention. During the emotional time, she overheard seven-year-old George tell a friend: "I can't play today because I have to be with my mother—she's so unhappy." Later, Barbara said that eventually she realized, "You either pull together or you shatter." She channeled her energy into her family and volunteer work with the Leukemia Society of America, the March of Dimes, and a forerunner of the Junior League, a women's service organization. Throwing herself into volunteer work, she established a thrift shop and spent hours soliciting donations. With the help of Jeb and both Georges, she was able to laugh again.

In time the family fell back into its old rhythms. George's business grew. According to *Who's Who*, he became the cofounder and director of Zapata Petroleum Company in 1953, the year Robin died, and three years later president of the Zapata Off Shore Company. His success helped support the large family both he and Barbara wanted. Neil Mallon Bush was born January 22, 1955, and Marvin Pierce Bush followed in October 1956. The Bushes continued their busy social life. While living in Midland, they moved twice and still found time to remain active, popular members of the community. David Hoffman of the *Washington Post* noted that after their years in Texas they had "more in common with the Lions Club [a civic service club] than the country club."

In 1959, the partners of Zapata Petroleum decided to split up their interconnected businesses and make each more independent. As the president of Zapata Off Shore, George chose to concentrate on offshore drilling and contracting. The decision involved moving across the state to the port city of Houston on the Gulf of Mexico, more than 400 miles east. Barbara, pregnant for the sixth time, packed up the family and looked forward to a new phase in life.

*Barbara and George and their four sons moved to Houston in 1959.
While George worked to make Zapata Off Shore Company a success,
Barbara cared for her sons and daughter Dorothy Walker Bush, who
was born on August 18, 1959.*

4

Entering the Arena

SHORTLY AFTER SETTLING in Houston in 1959, Barbara gave birth to a daughter, whom the Bushes named Dorothy Walker Bush, after George's mother. George began traveling again, to the Gulf of Mexico and other offshore drilling sites around the world. Barbara remained at home, tending to the new baby and the four rambunctious Bush sons. She and George continued to add to their wide circle of friends and were able to live well on George's earnings. Described as an "honest, industrious entrepreneur," George worked hard at making his company a success. At the same time, his sense of civic responsibility moved him toward activity in another arena.

Like his father, Prescott Bush, George was a member of the Republican party. While George was busy establishing his company and building his family, his father had become very active in Republican politics in Connecticut and had been elected senator in 1952, after failing two years earlier. Fitzhugh Green notes in his biography of George Bush that Prescott probably wanted to be president but had not begun his political career early enough for such an opportunity to present itself. He had concentrated on his career as a Wall Street banker, building financial security for his family. He did well as a senator, however, and remained in that office until 1963, when he retired.

The same year Prescott Bush began his successful campaign to become one of Connecticut's two senators, George became active in Texan Republican politics and worked on the first Eisenhower presidential campaign. Four years later, in 1956, he worked on Eisenhower's reelection campaign. When the Bushes moved to Houston, located in Harris County, George stepped up his interest in politics. In 1962, the Harris County Republican party asked him to join their candidate selection committee, which screened Republican candidates for office in the area. A short time later, the county party chairman resigned, and George was nominated for the vacant office. He enthusiastically began campaigning on weekends while continuing to run his drilling business during the week.

George's campaign brought a new role to Barbara—that of the political wife. She accompanied him everywhere during his run, which included visits to all 189 precincts in Harris County. She appeared at local functions, got to know the various people involved in politics at the county level, and worked with volunteers distributing literature. Her intuition about people became a campaign asset. Barbara recalled the campaign as the "hottest, meanest race" George ever entered, but despite the unfamiliar atmosphere and hard work, she threw herself into campaigning. Years later, she indulged in some self-deprecating humor with a *Life* magazine writer when she claimed, "The first time I campaigned, I probably lost George hundreds of votes." Barbara was probably exaggerating, for George won the race and became chairman of the Harris County Republican organization. When he did so, Barbara realized that in addition to being the wife of a socially prominent businessman and the well-organized mother of five, she had to put her skills and personality to work as a politician's wife.

Her support and enthusiasm were necessary to George, for he faced a daunting task as a Republican leader in Texas, where the electorate was predominantly Democratic. In 1963, the year he was elected chairman, the nation's popular young Democratic president, John F. Kennedy, was assassinated in Dallas and the vice-president, Lyndon Johnson, succeeded him. Johnson was a native Texan and an excellent politician. As president, his support for Texan Democratic candidates carried quite a bit of weight. George had to work hard at bolstering the Republican party there.

While he spent time working for the Republican organization and managing Zapata Off Shore, Barbara was often home alone with the children. Her daughter Dorothy later spoke about that period with Ann Grimes. She

Barbara and George get the election results for the 1964 Senate primaries over the phone. George became the Republican candidate for the Senate seat, and Barbara helped him in his campaign by canvassing voters and hostessing parties.

During the 1964 campaign, Barbara (second from right) and George attend the First Pink Elephant Ball, a fundraising event given by the Republican Women's Club in Midland, Texas.

recalled, "When I would tell her about problems with my kids, I remember Mom saying she spent so many lonely, lonely hours with us kids. She'd say stuff like 'You weren't *that* fascinating at age two.' I can understand how she felt. She did it all. She brought us up." Dorothy went on to say that her father was often there for the children, but the burden of child raising rested firmly on Barbara's shoulders. Barbara stood up to the many demands placed on her, allowing George to confidently devote his energy to politics and business.

George's efforts gained him a measure of prominence, and in 1964 he was asked to run as the Republican candidate for the U.S. Senate against the Democratic incumbent, Ralph Yarborough. Despite his growing popularity, he was just beginning to hone his political skills. Outside of Odessa, Midland, and Houston, the response to a rousing cry of "George Bush for Senator!" was likely to be "George Who?" To make himself better known, he took on a grueling campaign schedule, and Barbara was there to sustain him. According to Radcliffe, Barbara's effort included canvassing voters door-to-door while identified only by a name tag that said "Barbara" so no one would know she was the candidate's wife and that way she could get "an honest opinion of George." She campaigned hard, was a gracious hostess, and rarely forgot a name or face. With experience, her poise, style, and confidence grew.

Both nominees played political hardball to win the Senate seat. Despite the 16 years George had spent living and developing his business in Texas, he was branded a "carpetbagger"—a derogatory term, popular among southerners in the post–Civil War era, that referred to northerners who came south to get elected. The personal attacks even extended to Barbara's father, Marvin Pierce, who oversaw the publication of a number of magazines, including *Redbook*. In a bizarre accusation, members of the extremely conservative John Birch Society claimed that *Redbook*, a women's magazine that contained tips on homemaking, child raising, and cooking, was actually an

An informal moment with the Bush family before the election of 1964. Despite the 16 years George had spent living in Texas, he was called a "carpetbagger" by his opponents during the campaign.

official publication of the Communist party (members of which were referred to as "Reds"). The personal slurs flew.

When the election results came in after the long, exhausting campaign, George had 43.6 percent of the vote—not enough to win. Although he lost the race for the Senate seat, he had received more votes than any other Republican candidate in Texas history. He and Barbara knew it was at least a respectable showing, but five-year-old Dorothy was bewildered by the news. She told her parents she was sad because she would be "the only one in school who has a father without a job." She need not have worried. Although her father did not have the job he wanted, his drilling business kept him busy and provided amply for the family's needs.

His unsuccessful 1964 run for the Senate taught George and Barbara a great deal about the enormous amounts of time and energy required to run a campaign. George began to question his commitments and wondered if he could be successful as a congressional candidate while running the Zapata Off Shore Company. In 1965, while he assessed his next political move, the congressional districts for members of the U.S. House of Representatives from Texas were reapportioned, creating a new seat to represent the Seventh

George raises his fingers in a sign of hopeful victory before he and Barbara cast their ballots in the 1964 elections. Although George received more votes than any other Republican candidate ever had in Texas history, he lost the election to the Democratic incumbent, Ralph Yarborough.

District in Houston. In February 1966, George declared his candidacy for the new position.

He also sold Zapata Off Shore for a reported $1.1 million so that he could devote his full time to the pursuit of elected office. In his autobiography, George related that he did not have to explain to Barbara why he wanted to sell his lucrative business to run for a job that in 1966 paid $18,000 a year. He noted, "She shared my concern for the way things were going in the country and my feeling that we had an obligation to put something back into a society that had given us so much." The nation was in a period of upheaval. The problems of civil rights, racial equality, poverty, urban blight, and the escalating conflict in Vietnam generated a wide range of divisive opinions among Americans. George felt he ought to do his part to lead and represent the people who shared his views of the best solution to the nation's problems. Also, running Zapata no longer provided him with the challenge it once did. He believed that there were "more important ways to contribute to our children's future. Going to Washington as a member of Congress was a step in that direction." Of course, the first step was to win the election.

By that point, George and Barbara were more seasoned campaigners. The campaign team was highly organized and well financed. Barbara again worked very hard to help her husband in his bid for the post. Whenever possible, she was at his side at meetings and rallies. She sent a handwritten letter to the district's women voters outlining George's virtues and explaining that "George loves his God, his family, his friends, and his fellow man." As the campaign wore on, it became apparent that the voters loved George. He garnered 57.6 percent of the vote, defeating his Democratic opponent Frank Briscoe, the district attorney of Harris County. The Republican victory was particularly impressive because Harris County had six times as many Democrats as Republicans among its registered voters.

The Bush family was once again headed for a new home. Their move to Washington, D.C., was their 15th in 22 years. George looked forward to the exciting political life of the nation's capital; Barbara eagerly anticipated going back east after 18 years in Texas. She realized a new phase in their life together was beginning.

Barbara and George prepared themselves and their 5 children, who ranged in age from 19-year-old George W. to 6-year-old Dorothy, for the move to Washington. George launched himself into the endless work of a congressman. Barbara applied her enormous energy and organizational skills to settling her children into a new life. As a veteran of many moves, even buying a house over the telephone did not daunt her. During a conversation with Senator Milward Simpson (whose son Alan also became a senator), she purchased a house on Hillbrook Lane in northwest Washington. George W. went to New Haven, Connecticut, where he began course work at Yale University, as his father and grandfather had done. Barbara enrolled the other children in local private schools. The transition from the freewheeling environment of Texas to sophisticated metropolitan Washington provided them all with a challenge, especially 11-year-old Neil, who was teased about his heavy Texas accent, crew-cut hair, and liking for white socks. In a short time, though, they adjusted, and once again numerous friends filled the Bush home.

The Bushes' friends were soon introduced to their new backyard as Barbara began hosting regular Sunday barbecues. This custom was a continuation of the informal style and warm hospitality Barbara was known for in Texas. Washington was filled with old friends from Yale, Andover, business, and politics. Frequent guests of the Bushes included Wisconsin congressman William Steiger and his wife, Janet, and Supreme Court Justice Potter Stewart and his wife Mary Ann, known as Andy. They and other friends enjoyed helping themselves to soup, chili,

Barbara and George beam with delight following George's victory in the 1966 race for a seat representing the Seventh District in the U.S. House of Representatives. During the campaign, Barbara had written a letter to the woman voters explaining that George was the right man for the job.

hamburgers cooked by George on the outdoor grill (even in winter), and ice cream on a stick. Conversation ranged widely, and they discussed real estate, sports, and politics. In this comfortable setting, Barbara felt free to tell stories and to use her skills at mimicry to describe her experiences. Andy Stewart commented that when Barbara was among trusted friends, her sense of humor was "killing." Both George and Barbara quickly established friendships that they have maintained over time. Their son Marvin commented in a January 10, 1989, *People* magazine article, "When you become a friend of the Bushes', you're a friend for life."

Guests were made to feel like part of the family, and Barbara never knew how many to expect. Their son Marvin later described to Fitzhugh Green the happy but chaotic environment in the house on Sunday afternoons. He told his father's biographer that George would go out to run errands or to the store, run into an acquaintance, and invite him or her over for the barbecue. Often, without warning, he would return with three or four more people. Before Barbara knew it, she would have more than 20 hungry guests in the backyard. She completely accepted George's easygoing ways and became expert at entertaining with a minimum of notice and fuss. George appreciated her skills as a hostess and did not hesitate to invite important constituents from Texas home for dinner. Although their circle of friends grew ever larger, Barbara and George preferred their own informal style and tended to avoid the Washington social whirl.

Barbara developed her own network of friends through organizations and groups that welcomed congressional newcomers and their family members to Washington— groups such as the 90th Club and SOS, a group of Yale and Harvard alumni who were moderate Republicans. She soon became a Washington insider. Her sense of fun and down-to-earth personality immediately drew people to her. She went out of her way to include friends in her activities, whether it was an outing to a garden show or an afternoon visit to the National Gallery. Members of her circle kidded her by claiming that she had about 2,000 best friends. Still, she always found time for her family. Barbara loved to take her children on tours of the capital, which has more sites listed on the National Register of Historic Places than any other U.S. city, and she also took time to practice photography.

Whenever she heard of a friend in need, Barbara reached out to help. To come to the aid of one woman who had locked herself out of her house, Barbara climbed through a window and opened a door. Mindful of how her neighbors in Texas had rallied around when Robin was ill, when sickness or death touched a friend, Barbara did all she could to help the family through the crisis. She often helped Texans moving to Washington to get settled. Her sister-in-law, Nancy Ellis, spoke with Radcliffe about Barbara's outgoing nature: "Barbara is freed up to go and do wonderful things because she's not bottled up worrying about how does so-and-so feel about me or how do I feel about them." She told Radcliffe that Barbara just did not

The Jefferson Memorial is located at the Tidal Basin in Washington, D.C. In 1966, after George won a seat in the U.S. House of Representatives, the Bushes moved to the nation's capital. Barbara often toured many of the city's landmarks, such as the Jefferson Memorial, with her children.

have a lot of complicated relationships to bog her down. Barbara calls herself "a good friend, a loyal friend." When Radcliffe asked Barbara what she looked for in a friend, she replied: "I don't look for anything. I often find loyalty, humor, goodness. Hope they find the same from me."

In addition to taking care of the children and entertaining their friends, Barbara helped her husband directly by writing a monthly update about Washington for his Houston constituents. He was extremely busy and spent much time commuting between his offices on Capitol Hill and in the Seventh District. He did well, and Wilbur Mills, the Democratic chairman of the Ways and Means Committee and an old friend of Prescott Bush's, appointed him to the powerful Ways and Means Committee, which is responsible for all tax and revenue bills. The appointment marked the first time in 60 years that a freshman (first-term) representative from either party had been called to join the committee. Because of his increasing political commitments, George relied on Barbara to be the mainstay of the family. When possible, he spent his free weekend time individually with the children, but the rest of the time Barbara was firmly in control.

The Bushes' son Jeb chose to describe the family as if
it were a corporation: "Dad was the chief executive officer,
but Mother was the chief operating officer. We reported to
her. She did a good job keeping the family intact." When
the house on Hillbrook Lane proved to lack the space the
family needed, in 1968 she found a new house on Palisade
Lane, which once again became the hub of the neighbor-
hood children. Often 10 to 15 people could be found
wandering in and out of the house. Although the situation
could appear chaotic, Barbara had established straightfor-
ward rules and codes of conduct. According to Marvin, the
worst offenses were to pick on or make fun of someone,
take advantage of another's weaknesses, hurt someone's
feelings, renege on your word, or be "swell-headed." The
Bush children were taught to be firm but polite and tactful
when expressing opinions. She also taught the children not
to lie to her under any circumstances. In an interview
published in *Woman's Day* magazine in October 1990,
Barbara recommended telling a child: "I know when
you're lying, so don't bother to lie. I can always tell." She
added, "You almost always can."

Although Barbara was the "enforcer," as Neil told
Radcliffe, George was the "ultimate authority whenever
there was a conflict which couldn't be resolved at the mom
level." As Marvin pointed out, dealing with a house filled
with teenagers was not exactly "dealing with a handful of
saints." Barbara admitted in her interview with *Women's
Day* that she sometimes "sounded like a wicked witch"
when disciplining the children. However, they never took
her threats too seriously. But they all understood the clearly stated rules of the house, which included compulsory
Sunday church attendance and strict observance of cur-
fews, which occasionally obliged the boys to be at home
earlier than their dates. Barbara recalled that when a rule
was broken, George could devastate the transgressor merely by telling the child how disappointed he was. When
George and Barbara did not agree on something concern-

ing their children, they would come to a decision after speaking together privately and then present a united front.

Both George and Barbara valued the advice Marvin Pierce had given them about raising children, which Barbara repeated to Trude Feldman in a September 1988 interview in *McCall's* magazine: "Children should be given lots of love and be shown good examples, in addition to being taught honesty and to follow the work ethic." Both George and Barbara have a strong religious faith, and both have taught Sunday school. They strove to instill traditional religious values in their children. Because the family had always been wealthy, the Bushes were also careful to teach the children—by their example of helping others through their church, school, charities, and public service—that they had an obligation to give to others because they had been given so much themselves. "Giving back" unobtrusively is one of the most deeply held Bush family values.

George remained in his congressional seat after the 1968 election. But 2 years later, at the age of 46, he decided to try again for a Senate seat. His Democratic opponent Lloyd Bentsen, Jr. was very popular, and even Prescott Bush, who had retired from office, urged George not to run. After a hard-fought race, Bentsen emerged with nearly

In 1969, President Richard Nixon (far right) shares the spotlight with Barbara and George as he makes a campaign appearance during George's run for a Senate seat in the 1970 elections. Despite support from the president, George lost the election to Lloyd Bentsen, Jr.

Barbara finds time to do needlepoint in the Waldorf Towers suite of the U.S. representative to the United Nations, where the Bushes resided from mid-1971 to late 1972. Barbara enjoyed being a diplomat's wife and admitted, "I'd pay to have this job."

150,000 more votes than Bush out of the total 2.2 million cast. In consolation, Republican president Richard Nixon sent George a telegram the day after the election. Nixon wrote: "From personal experience I know the disappointment that you and your family must feel at this time. I am sure, however, that you will not allow this defeat to discourage you in your effort to continue to provide leadership for our party and the nation."

At first, George and Barbara were discouraged. George had given up his safe seat in the House of Representatives to run for the Senate. Barbara, who had worked very hard on the campaign, found losing the election particularly

painful. She has admitted that she cries easily, whether she is happy or sad. When Nancy Ellis called her after hearing the election results, Barbara got on the phone and "couldn't stop crying." George returned to Washington to complete the last weeks of his term and make plans for the future. In his autobiography, he recalls reporters at a news conference at his district office in Houston asking how he felt about losing and what he might do next. He responded that "after you get over the initial hurt, the blow of losing, it's not so bad. The future doesn't look nearly as gloomy as it did eight hours ago."

The Bushes' gloom lifted entirely less than one month later, when President Nixon named George Bush the U.S. representative to the United Nations. The clan packed up again for yet another move. When George took office in March 1971, he, Barbara, Jeb, Neil, Marvin, and Dorothy moved into their quarters on the 42nd floor of the Waldorf Towers in New York City. (George W. Bush had followed in his father's footsteps and was serving in the armed forces, although he chose to enter the air force instead of the navy.) The Waldorf Towers was the site of the official residence of the U.S. representative to the UN, and the U.S. suite there consisted of three separate apartments converted into one. Living in a Manhattan high-rise was a new experience for Barbara, but she adapted quickly.

While George earned the respect of the diplomatic community for his abilty to learn rapidly and cultivate personal relationships with fellow delegates, Barbara enthusiastically threw herself into entertaining. Much UN business depends on congenial friendships and contacts among the delegates and their staff members, and dinners, receptions, and cocktail parties are essential elements of the social scene that allows such relationships to blossom. Barbara, already adept at informal entertaining, graciously responded to George's spur-of-the-moment invitations to members of the international community.

Barbara thrived as a diplomatic hostess. In a 1985 speech at American University in Washington, she described her life as a UN diplomat's wife. It was, she said, like "being taken around the world to meet people from a hundred twenty-eight countries, and yet never having to pack a bag or sleep in a strange bed." Unlike George, who had traveled widely for years as part of his business, Barbara had never been abroad. She managed to turn that fact, which could have been a drawback, into an asset by making the Waldorf Towers suite a showcase for what she knew best—the United States. She helped her many foreign guests become acquainted with their host country by showing only the works of U.S. artists, serving California and New York wines, and wearing clothing by U.S. designers. Her warm, outgoing manner was also an asset to George. His personal assistant, Rudolph "Foxy" Carter, told Fitzhugh Green how he would point a woman out to Barbara at a party, mention that she might be interesting to talk to, and briefly describe any difficulty the U.S. mission at the UN might be having with the country she and her husband represented. Barbara would accept an introduction to the person, chat with her, and take her and her husband to meet George, encouraging better international relations in the process. Carter praised their style as "gracious, professional teamwork." Radcliffe noted that the Bushes were "a smashing success" at the UN. But her duties as a diplomat's wife were not merely an obligation: Barbara admitted, "I'd pay to have this job."

The Bushes also enjoyed less formal events such as trips to Shea Stadium to watch Mets baseball games from George's uncle Herbert Walker's box, Sunday visits to George's parents' country home in nearby Greenwich, Connecticut, and dining at the exclusive Lynx Club in New York. George and Barbara always kept in touch with their old friends and frequently included people they knew from Washington in their activities.

When Barbara had free time, she attended open meetings of the UN Security Council and did needlepoint while listening to the debates. In memory of her daughter Robin, she devoted time to volunteer work at the Memorial Sloan-Kettering Cancer Center, and she spent her time there cheering up cancer patients during their difficult, painful treatments. Sadly, one of the patients was her father-in-law, Prescott Bush, who was admitted to the center suffering from a rapidly spreading case of lung cancer. Dorothy Bush, to whom Barbara was very close, stayed with Barbara and George in the Waldorf Towers and visited Prescott at the center until he died in October 1972.

About one month later, newly reelected President Nixon asked George to return to Washington and take over the chairmanship of the Republican National Committee. Barbara later told interviewer Michael Kilian that she told George he could "accept the job over my dead body. You're a statesman, stay out of that." She worried because the party chairman was necessarily embroiled in party politics, which could be nasty. Her misgivings proved justified.

In June 1972, members of the Committee to Re-Elect the President (CREEP) had engaged in a number of illegal activities in pursuit of their goal. They had hired burglars who had broken into the Democratic headquarters in the Watergate office complex in Washington, D.C., in search of useful material and records. What made Watergate, as the ensuing scandal came to be known, so shocking was that they had done so with the knowledge and approval of President Nixon, who then abused the powers of his office to thwart investigation into the incident and cover up the involvement of CREEP members.

Without knowing any of this, six months later in January 1973, George Bush took office as Republican National Committee chairman. He and Barbara continued to be popular members of the Washington political community

and resumed their practice of entertaining at home frequently. George and Barbara welcomed old friends to their
home, made new ones, and worked to strengthen the Republican party. But as revelations about Watergate came
to light, pleasant conversations in Washington were muted
by the growing suspicion, and finally, knowledge, that the
Republican president of the United States had broken the
law and lied to the American people to gain reelection.

During the early part of 1974, Nixon's presidency was
gradually dragged to its destruction. George tried to em-
phasize that the entire Republican party should not be held
accountable for the illegal activities of Nixon and his
cronies. Finally, as reported in Fitzhugh Green's book, on
August 7, 1974, George sent a letter to Nixon that said in
part: "It is my considered judgment that you should now
resign. . . . I now feel that the resignation is best for the
country, best for this President. I believe this view is held
by most Republican leaders across the country. This letter
is much more difficult because of the gratitude I will
always feel toward you." The next day, Nixon read his
formal letter of resignation to the American public on
national television. He was the first president in U.S.
history to resign, and he did so in disgrace. The nation
went through a period of bitter resentment toward its
leaders. Barbara later admitted to Radcliffe, "Nixon really
fooled us."

Upon Nixon's resignation, Vice-president Gerald Ford
took office. George was one of several candidates for the
now-vacant vice-presidency, but Nelson Rockefeller was
Ford's eventual choice. Unsurprisingly, George wanted to
leave his post as chairman of the Republican National
Committee and in his autobiography noted that both he and
Barbara wanted to get as far away as possible from the
nightmare of Watergate. Ford offered George his choice
of ambassadorships to London or Paris. George thought it
over and instead asked for a more challenging assign-
ment—that of U.S. envoy to the People's Republic of

China, which had cautiously begun diplomatic relations with the United States just one year earlier. Few Americans had visited China, which was run by the Communist party that had been founded by Mao Zedong. The Chinese were historically suspicious of Westerners, and the nation had treated both the Soviet Union and the United States as its enemies during its recent history. In 1972, President Nixon's groundbreaking visit to China—the first by a U.S. president—had finally made relations possible between the two huge nations.

George and Barbara were eager to be pioneers again, as they had been early in their marriage when they left the East for Texas. In October 1974 they departed for Beijing, China, where George was to head the 226-member staff of the U.S. Liaison Office. Barbara was thrilled. At the age of 49, after years of listening to stories of George's travels, seeing slides of friends' trips, and entertaining guests from around the world, she was finally setting off on her own foreign adventure.

In December 1975, the Bushes pose with President Gerald Ford (right), his wife, Betty, and their daughter, Susan, at the U.S. consulate in Peking (now Beijing). Barbara was ecstatic when President Ford offered George the position of U.S. chief liaison to China in 1974 because she was finally going to embark on her own foreign adventure.

Although the Bushes had a Chrysler sedan at their disposal during their time in China, they preferred the Chinese way to travel— bicycling.

5

Turning Points

WHEN BARBARA AND GEORGE LANDED in Beijing in 1974, China was just beginning to emerge from the turmoil of the Cultural Revolution and its isolation from the outside world. The Cultural Revolution was Mao's ill-fated effort to purge China of his rivals and reinvigorate the Communist leadership. During the 1960s, many doctors, engineers, professors, teachers, and others had been killed or persecuted at Mao's urging by enthusiastic young students called Red Guards. The Red Guards themselves soon grew too powerful for Mao's liking, and the former persecutors found themselves exiled from universities to distant farms to be "reeducated"—forced to work as rural laborers. After this destruction of its own talent, China of the 1970s was trying to reenter the 20th century by seeking scientific, commercial, and intellectual exchanges with the United States, although they did not open formal diplomatic relations. The liaison office George headed was only the second one ever in the history of Communist China and the United States. Years of suspicion and fear and a long-standing tradition of secrecy in government made it difficult for the office to schedule even routine courtesy calls with Chinese officials. Henry Kissinger, former secretary of state, warned George before he left that he would be bored by the lethargic Chinese government processes.

Forewarned, Barbara prepared by shipping, in her words, "enough needlepoint to stretch from here to Michigan, paints and oils, and every book I ever wanted to read." But Barbara was not bored in China. She plunged into life there wholeheartedly, studying the Chinese language, immersing herself in the culture, and spending much time with George. The envoy had the use of an official Chrysler sedan, but within a month George and Barbara were traveling as the Chinese people do—by bicycle. Guests at formal diplomatic parties were astonished to see the two Americans arrive on bicycles, for the previous liaison chief, David Bruce, had maintained a much more restrained, formal style. The Bushes liked bicycling because it afforded them wonderful exercise, but they also appreciated the feeling of freedom they gained.

The foreign representatives in Beijing were encased in a kind of cocoon, a different world far removed from that of the Chinese who surrounded them. The liaison office and the Bushes' residence were located in a walled compound guarded by Chinese soldiers of the People's Liberation Army. Even when the Bushes took a spin on their bicycles, a security guard followed them everywhere. To meet Chinese government officials the Bushes attended various national holiday receptions held by the other foreign embassies, thinking that if they could not meet the officials at the liaison office functions, perhaps they could see them at another country's affair. They tried to make contact with the Chinese people, but the language barrier was nearly insurmountable, and the Chinese government discouraged their people from talking to the Americans. But the Bushes' friendly style prevailed, and both recall how they "developed warmly reciprocated friendships with . . . official Chinese." Barbara and George also en-joyed sight-seeing excursions to the Great Wall, the tombs of the Qin and Ming dynasties, where thousands of life-size terra-cotta figures had been buried, and other spots deemed to be of interest by the Chinese government.

The "attention" the government showed the Bushes is well illustrated by a story Barbara told. During an official visit by Henry Kissinger, the Bushes stayed in a govern-ment-run guest house just outside Beijing. The house was provided with nearly everything they might need: bath-robes, slippers, notepaper, pens, ink, cosmetics, tooth-paste, and toothbrushes. After Barbara wrote a letter there, she mentioned to George and John Holdridge, his deputy, that their hosts had provided everything but the glue for stamps. Only the three Americans were in the room. The next morning, a bottle of glue sat on Barbara's desk—and neither George nor Holdridge had put it there.

Despite the constant surveillance, the Bushes' stay in China was their first opportunity in a long while to spend time together alone. They were far from the activities that had filled their days in Washington and New York. Bar-bara told interviewer Dan Oberdorfer in December 1974 that life in Beijing was very different. In Washington and New York, the telephone seemed to ring all day long. When George came home, he would be on the phone again in the evening. During their first five weeks in Beijing, George received two telephone calls, excluding Barbara's. She told Oberdorfer that she tried to call George once a day because "I think he misses the phone as much as anything." For her part, Barbara quickly made friends with the British wife of the Argentine ambassador, Maureen O'Ryan, and the two frequently made trips together to visit the Ming tombs outside Beijing.

The Bushes' day began at 7:00 A.M., when they listened to a summary of world news on the Voice of America program. (Voice of America is the radio division of the U.S. Information Agency and broadcasts world news,

These life-size terra-cotta warriors from the Qin dynasty stand guard over an emperor's tomb. Bar-bara and George visited the Qin Tombs, near Xian, on their numerous sight-seeing tours of China.

George and Barbara often hosted dinners in Beijing to honor various officials, such as the one pictured here for President Yang Shangkur (standing between the Bushes). In an attempt to bring a bit of American culture to China, the menu contained Texas-style barbecue.

among other programs, in 44 languages to all parts of the world.) Breakfast was fresh yogurt served in returnable jars from a Chinese shop. Just a few steps away from their house was the liaison office, where George spent the morning. At 11:40 both George and Barbara received an hour-long Chinese lesson, followed by a lunch of many courses, the main meal of the day. The days were quiet and much the same, at least until the Bushes tired of the pace and began inviting friends, politicians, administration officials, and relatives from overseas to Beijing. In 1976, Barbara told a reporter from the *Houston Post* that she had "wall-to-wall guests" because George was forever inviting people to visit. One invitee, Charles Whitehouse, then U.S. ambassador to Thailand, recalled: "George asked me casually one day to come see him. It took almost two weeks of travel time to stay one week with Bush in China" because the flight had to be routed through Tokyo. Another group of visitors was headed by Senator Charles Percy of Illinois, with whom the Bushes were friendly. He led the first U.S. congressional delegation ever to visit Communist China, and the Bushes happily welcomed the crowd, which included Senator Jacob Javits of New York and Senator Claiborne Pell of Rhode Island.

Another eyewitness to the Bushes' stay in China was C. Fred Bush, a cocker spaniel named after an old friend from Texas and given to Barbara by her son Marvin. Barbara has always loved dogs, and since her childhood in Rye, she has never been without one. Getting C. Fred to Beijing required some maneuvering, and Barbara made sure to ask for permission before she brought him with her. She had little idea of how strongly the Chinese people would react. After the Communists won the bloody civil war in the 1940s, China was devastated. Dogs, believed to spread disease, were exterminated and so became an unfamiliar sight to a generation of Chinese. The appearance of C. Fred trotting along on the end of a leash held by Barbara elicited surprise, curiosity, and fear. Some Chinese pointed at him and called him "cat." Barbara quickly learned to say in Chinese, "Don't worry, he's only a little dog and he doesn't bite." Just as the people of Beijing were surprised to see C. Fred ambling down the sidewalk, the Bushes were surprised after eating a certain course at a ceremonial dinner. A staff member explained that the "fragrant meat" they had just been served was correctly translated "the upper lip of a wild dog." Evidently, not all the dogs had been exterminated, after all.

For the first time since her marriage, Barbara did not spend Christmas with George. She went to the United States to be with the children, and Dorothy Bush visited her son in China. But during the summer of 1975, all of the Bush children except Jeb managed to make it to Beijing. Jeb, 22 years old, had just married Columba Garnica and begun a new job at the Texas Commerce Bank and could not get time off. George W., who was 29 years old,

During the summer of 1975, all of the Bush children, photographed here with Barbara and George in 1980, managed to visit their parents in China, with the exception of Jeb (back row, holding his son George), who had just started a new job and could not get time off from work.

graduated from Harvard Business School and was planning to enter the oil industry in Texas; 20-year-old Neil was at Tulane University in New Orleans; and Marvin, a year younger than Neil, was entering the University of Virginia in September. Dorothy celebrated her 16th birthday on the trip by being christened at the Beijing Chongwenmen Christian Church, where Sunday services in Chinese were conducted for a congregation of about 10 diplomats and 4 aged Chinese. (Communist China was officially atheist and discouraged the practice of its own traditional religions of Buddhism, Confucianism, and Taoism, as well as Christianity.) The Bushes thought the tiny church would be a very special place for a ceremony long overdue, and when the service was over, the minister told Dorothy that she was now a lifetime member of the little church.

The Bushes' exotic interlude in China ended in December 1975. President Gerald Ford offered George the opportunity to take on the job of director of the Central Intelligence Agency (CIA). Barbara did not encourage him to accept. Both worried that the position might be a political "dead end street," and Barbara remembered how hard the Watergate years had been on the children. She feared having a father who headed the CIA would be even harder for them. But George accepted, and they left China in December, when George returned to appear before the Senate during hearings to confirm his appointment. In January 1976 he was sworn in by his old neighbor and friend, Supreme Court justice Potter Stewart. The difference in his life was dramatic; he faced a job like none he had ever done before. The changes were to profoundly affect Barbara as well.

In several interviews, Barbara has mentioned how much George has shared with her over the years. She stressed in a 1988 *McCall's* interview that the sense of sharing has made their marriage as successful as it is, saying, "George includes me and makes me a part of his life, and I like that very much." But when George was director of the CIA, he could not share much having to do with the position: Most of what he did was highly confidential. Barbara sat in their home on Palisade Lane, guarded by secret agents who monitored every visitor and recorded the license plate number of every car that passed. The house was empty. Children no longer filled it, no political campaign required her energy, and she had no diplomatic role as a hostess. The emotional letdown led to a serious depression. For many years, she never spoke to anyone about the episode. George tried to "gut it out" with her, as she later put it, and reassured her of the value and importance of all she had done. Frequently she cried without reason. As she contemplated her life, she thought about the emerging women's movement and later said she felt pressured by it. In the *Woman's Day* interview she said, "I think that a lot of wives and mothers of my generation woke up one day and felt we hadn't accomplished anything because we weren't in the workplace."

She managed to work her way out of the depression and filled her time by volunteering at a local hospice–nursing home two or three days a week and by assembling a slide show on her experiences in China. She presented the show at lectures she held, raised thousands of dollars, and donated the money to her church in Houston. Gradually, her gloom lifted, but in later years, she looked back on 1976 as her "wasted year." In *Running Mates*, Grimes quotes a long conversation Barbara had with her on a flight back to Washington in 1988. She said, in part, "I later mentioned it [her depression] to a doctor friend and he said, 'Well, why didn't you come for help?' I said, 'I wouldn't have thought of that.'" She added, "But I'm very sympathetic to people who have a depression now. It's a physical pain."

In November 1976, Jimmy Carter, the Democratic candidate for president, won the election. As a high-ranking Republican appointed by the outgoing Republican administration, George realized he had to leave his post at the CIA. He and Barbara left Washington and returned to Houston. For the first time since 1948, George did not have a job, but before long both he and Barbara were busier than ever.

When the Bushes moved back to Houston in January 1977, their life together moved into a new phase. For the first time since their marriage in 1945, they were on their own. George W., Neil, and Jeb were involved in their own careers. Marvin and Dorothy were away at college most of the time. George had no business or political commitments—but he had great ambitions.

George launched himself into a number of undertakings. He became a board member of four corporations, invested in a partnership with Robert Mosbacher to buy oil transport barges, and involved himself in a number of community

activities. His long record of public service continued with his work as a director of Baylor Medical College in Texas; as a trustee of his high school alma mater, Phillips Academy, and of Trinity University in San Antonio; and as chairman of the American Heart Fund. He also accepted a position as an adjunct professor at Rice University. Somehow he had time left for extensive travel, and he and Barbara visited Hong Kong, Australia, Singapore, Iran, Jordan, Egypt, Israel, Greece, and Denmark. They revisited China and were allowed to enter the nation of Tibet, long isolated by the Himalayas and more recently by its government. Barbara was only the third American woman to officially visit that remote nation.

Throughout this busy period, George was quietly promoting the idea of a presidential campaign. He spoke frequently and maintained the large network of friends and political contacts he had built over the years. He had carefully observed how President Jimmy Carter had used

In 1976, George Bush is sworn in as director of the Central Intelligence Agency (CIA) by Supreme Court Justice Potter Stewart as Barbara and President Ford look on. George's tenure as CIA director marked the beginning of a period that Barbara remembers as her "wasted year" because she could no longer share in her husband's work, which was highly confidential.

a grass-roots campaign—gathering support from local and state politicians who knew him well—to win the Democratic presidential nomination in 1976 and then capture the presidency. As time passed, George considered the Carter administration a failure and thought Carter would lose his bid for a second term. He prepared to establish his own campaign for the office, and with the aid of James Baker, manager of the Ford presidential campaign in 1976, he established the Fund for a Limited Government as a source of campaign money. George's confidence grew as contributions to the fund increased.

For six weeks in the summer of 1978, George met with groups of domestic and foreign policy experts at the Bush summer home in Kennebunkport, Maine. The advisers spent time with George discussing his political prospects and positions, while Barbara divided her time between attending briefing sessions and ensuring the comfort of the guests by arranging clambakes, lobster feeds, and accommodations. She also devoted a great deal of thought to how she could use the visibility inherent in being a candidate's wife to publicize her volunteer activities. She had to decide on a focus that would be politically appropriate for the wife of a potential president.

Barbara was at a turning point in thinking about herself and how to support George's campaign. Her time in China with George had given her a new sense of confidence. In *Running Mates* she is quoted as saying: "I think it just taught me that I could be good. I don't think that I was not confident before, but I would say that I was, you know, C+ in confidence. I was perfectly happy living in my own little family spot." She knew she would have to stop living in her "little family spot" when George announced his candidacy. Presidential races hurl a candidate's entire family into a pressure cooker of endless campaigning and relentless media exposure. But as a veteran of several campaigns and bolstered by her hard-earned confidence, Barbara recognized that she was being presented not only with a challenge but also with an opportunity. She could publicize a special interest of her own, although she realized it had to complement, or at least not contradict, George's political positions. She reflected on the social problems that beset the United States: teen pregnancy, drug abuse, pollution, unemployment, and crime. After careful consideration, she decided that many of the nation's social ills were a consequence of illiteracy. She concluded that "having a more literate America would help almost everything."

Since her childhood, Barbara has loved to read. Her son Neil suffered from dyslexia, a reading disorder, and she experienced firsthand the frustrations he faced. Although many have traced her interest in literacy to her experience with Neil, in a July 1989 *Newsweek* interview she noted that this was not the case. After a lifetime of volunteer work she had thoughtfully chosen a cause to be identified with on the national level. She considered several issues too controversial; she just did not warm up to others. Literacy touched a wide range of social problems in a nonpolitical way and genuinely suited her interests and experience. Advancing the cause of literacy became the keystone of her public profile.

On May 1, 1979, George announced his candidacy at the National Press Club in Washington, D.C., with Barbara and his family by his side. The presidential election would not be held until November 1980, but the U.S. electoral process begins many months before an election. First, each party has to select its presidential candidate, which officially happens at the national conventions but actually is the result of months of primary elections. In both the Democratic and Republican parties, each state sends a certain number of delegates to the national convention, and how those delegates vote is determined by the votes in each party's primary elections in each state. More than half a dozen candidates may vie for their party's nomination during primaries. George had to prepare to campaign for Republican votes in many different states. The process was

Barbara speaks with children at an elementary school in Philadelphia. George's run for president in 1980 gave Barbara the opportunity to campaign for an interest of her own— literacy.

George and his son Marvin rejoice over George's defeat of Ronald Reagan in the Iowa precinct caucuses in January 1980. Barbara and her children worked tirelessly to help George in his campaign for the presidency.

long and grueling and involved months of strategy, fund-raising, and campaigning.

His speech at the National Press Club was not an auspicious beginning to the race and did not fire up either the audience or the press. Jack Germond and Jules Witcover, then working for the now-defunct *Washington Star*, wrote that George's campaign was the first in history to peak before it was even announced. Clearly the family had a lot of work to do. The first campaign trip followed George's speech and included visits to 10 cities in Connecticut, Massachusetts, New Hampshire, Vermont, Maine, Florida, and Alabama in the course of 4 days.

Barbara and the Bush children worked overtime during the campaign. Barbara's support of literacy programs gained media attention, and she promised to concentrate her energies on literacy and volunteerism as first lady. Ruth Graves, the president of Reading Is Fundamental (RIF), and Margaret McNamara, the wife of former secretary of defense Robert McNamara, were so impressed by Barbara's dedication that they invited her to become a RIF board member, regardless of the election results. Barbara accepted and was soon influential in unifying literacy groups, but "always quietly, never with any big show," according to her old friend Janet Steiger.

The first primary is held in Iowa, and George came in first place there, garnering the greatest number of votes. During the early part of the campaign, real momentum appeared to be building. In his autobiography, George called the 1980 run a "kind of ordeal by pressure cooker." Candidates are driven to look presidential throughout an unrelenting swirl of primaries, speeches, debates, interviews, and meetings. Although George spent 328 days on the road campaigning during the year following his announcement, Ronald Reagan, former president of the Screen Actors Guild and former governor of California, won the 1980 Republican presidential nomination.

At the Republican National Convention, held in Detroit, Michigan, in 1980, speculation about Reagan's choice of vice-presidential running mate filled the air, for the presidential candidate bore the main responsibility for the choice. Former president Gerald Ford was rumored to be the front runner. Tension ran high. Barbara and a group of Bush supporters were gathered in the Bush suite in the Hotel Pontchartrain when George received a call from Ronald Reagan, who said, "I'd like to go over to the convention and announce that you're my choice for vice-president. . . . If that's all right with you." George answered, "I'd be honored, Governor," and joyous bedlam erupted in the Bush suite. After a year of intense competition, Bush and Reagan joined forces. In November 1980, the Reagan-Bush ticket soundly defeated the Carter-Mondale ticket. George and Barbara headed back to Washington, and Barbara prepared to really go to work.

Left to right: Gerald Ford, Ronald Reagan, and George Bush appear together at the 1980 Republican National Convention held in Detroit, Michigan. Despite George's and Barbara's heavy campaigning, Reagan won the Republican presidential nomination. Soon after, Reagan invited George to be his vice-presidential running mate.

In 1988, on the presidential campaign trail, Barbara, George, and a large part of the Bush clan wave from the riverboat Natchez *upon their arrival at the Republican National Convention in New Orleans.*

6

In the Shadow of the White House

THE VICE-PRESIDENT'S HOUSE is a 33-room Victorian mansion that was built in 1893 and was for many years the home of naval admirals. Located on the parklike grounds of the Naval Observatory in northwest Washington, the house provides a kind of privacy unavailable at the White House, which is just a few miles away. Barbara enjoyed living there; she was able to take long walks with her dog and to garden when she had the time.

To help with writing official correspondence and planning activities, both the first lady and the wife of the vice-president maintain a small staff. According to an article in the October 1988 issue of *Ladies Home Journal*, Barbara dedicated about 50 percent of her time to literacy projects and to local charitable institutions, such as the Washington Home, a facility for the terminally ill where she regularly volunteers. Once a week she met with the wives of senators to help the American Red Cross, the Children's Hospital, and other institutions. But she was careful about not upstaging First Lady Nancy Reagan for public atten-

Barbara gardens when she visits the summer home in Kennebunkport, Maine. While living in the vice-president's house, which is located in the parklike area of the Naval Observatory in Washington, D.C., she enjoyed spending time planting flowers there, too.

tion. Barbara disliked comparisons between the two of them and told Radcliffe that "she and I are not alike and you can't compare apples and oranges, or whatever. And that doesn't take away from my enormous respect for her, and the job she's doing." Radcliffe also described Barbara as a "loyal Second Lady who never forgot her place." However, despite all statements to the contrary, the Reagans and the Bushes did not seem to enjoy the closeness that marked many of the Bushes' other political friendships.

The Bushes' style of entertaining during the vice-presidential years was never overly formal. Guests usually experienced a visit from one of Barbara's dogs—either C. Fred (who died in January 1987) or Millie (who joined the Bush family in February 1987). Millie liked to run into rooms holding a tennis ball in her mouth. During one formal dinner, Millie raced into the dining room, dropped a ball at the feet of the guest of honor, the Prime Minister of Australia, and stood there wagging her tail, expecting him to play. Barbara joked to Radcliffe, "I gave her a clean one in honor of the prime minister."

Barbara would occasionally bend the rules of protocol (rules that determine formal sitting arrangements and etiquette for the diplomatic corps and others at official social events); for example, she would not insist on having the guest of honor sit at her table, especially if the official visit was brief. She told Radcliffe: "This poor man didn't come to the United States to sit next to me. So I'll try to put him at the table with George so they can talk. I always make it clear that this is not the Vice President's idea, and they're very nice about it." Barbara's style could even be more relaxed. One afternoon while at a tea, she demonstrated to a group of women—wearing her silk dress and heels—how to use her exercise bike. Barbara is also known to have occassionally served popcorn as an hors d'oeuvre when entertaining.

The vice-president's house was the scene of nonstop entertaining by the Bushes. During the 8 years they lived in the house, they hosted more than 1,100 receptions. As Barbara later told Grimes, "We entertain a lot at our house. We have lunches, teas, coffees, breakfasts, dinners, and receptions, receptions, receptions." As a general rule, the press was excluded from these events because the Bushes defined them as "private" or "off the record" and therefore closed to reporters.

Unlike Nancy Reagan, who was roasted by the press for her $200,000 purchase of new china for the White House, Barbara supervised the redecoration of the vice-president's house, which cost about $124,000, without being criticized. Both the china fund and the redecorating fund had come from tax-deductible donations by private contributors. Within hours of an Associated Press report that made the fund known publicly, Barbara announced that no more contributions for the fund would be sought. The press did not pursue the story much further.

Somehow, in the middle of all her work as an official hostess and volunteer, Barbara found time to write a book. *C. Fred's Story*, published in 1984, was an "as told to" narrative about the experiences that Barbara's golden cocker spaniel, C. Fred, had while living with the vice-president's family. Inspiration for the book came from the people who wrote to C. Fred whenever his picture appeared in the newspapers. Barbara replied to the letters by signing the dog's name, until her chief of staff suggested that she put together a book. Lisa Drew, who was an editor at Doubleday and Company at the time, worked with Barbara to produce the book. It was written by Barbara in the voice of the dog and was "largely unchanged" by the editing process. The book has 62 photographs of C. Fred to help tell the story of his travels with the Bushes to such places as China, Texas, Maine, New York, and Washington. Elizabeth St. John, Doubleday's publicity manager, said the message of the book was "that celebraties are just like us. They have dogs that they spoil and they love just like we do. In that sense, *C. Fred's Story* is a very intimate book." Barbara made public appearances to promote the book, which became a successful seller and raised about $40,000 in royalities—all of which were donated to various literacy projects.

In 1984, after four years in office, President Reagan and Vice-President Bush faced election challenges from the Democratic nominees, Walter Mondale and Geraldine Ferraro (the first female candidate for the office of vice-president). Barbara again worked hard to promote the Reagan-Bush ticket. She was not pleased, however, with the harsh personal attacks that were hurled at her husband. Everything about him seemed to be criticized, from what he wore to how much money he had. During a public debate, Ferraro and Bush continued to verbally attack each other. The always proper, yet fiercely loyal, Barbara found herself uncomfortably pursued by the media, and a remark that she made to reporters during a trip to New York set off a blitz of publicity, causing her enormous distress and embarrassment. Thinking she was speaking "off the record" about some of the attacks made by Ferraro on her husband, she referred to Ferraro as a "$4 million—I can't say it, but it rhymes with rich." After the story broke, Barbara told Radcliffe that she cried for 24 hours and quickly apologized for the comment. There are so few instances in which Barbara says anything controversial that this rare example received a lot of media coverage. If anything, the incident demonstrates the unrelenting pressure and scrutiny that candidates and their families must confront daily. Barbara's unfortunate remark had no discernible effect on the outcome of the campaign—the Reagan-Bush ticket won a landslide victory on election day, and Barbara and George continued their way of life at the vice-president's house for another four years.

During the eight years that her husband served as vice-president, Barbara had shown what John Ensor Harr in the December 1988 issue of the *Saturday Evening Post* called "missionary fervor" in her dedication to literacy. She gave speeches throughout the country, visited volunteer tutors and new readers, and really helped to shape what has become a national literacy movement. Democrats and Republicans alike praise her contributions. Her continuing efforts reflect the importance of what she calls "giving back." She also told Harr, "Some people give time, some money, some their skills and connections, some literally have given their life's blood . . . but everyone has something to give." Barbara continued her comments about literacy work, explaining, "I honestly don't know of a more important gift anyone can give than the gift of literacy."

As part of a three-hour Fourth of July special on ABC-TV in 1988 that promoted the cause of literacy by way of a celebration of the Bicentennial of the Constitution, Barbara agreed to speak about the need to overcome illiteracy. She was to introduce J. T. Pace, the 63-year-old son of a former sharecropper from South Carolina, who had recently overcome a lifetime of illiteracy. Pace was scheduled to read the Preamble of the Constitution to 800,000 people who had gathered at the Gateway Arch in St. Louis, Missouri. Shortly before he was about to speak, Pace announced that he could not do the reading. He was introduced to Barbara, who sat and talked to him. She quickly realized how nervous he was and told him that she and every other reader sometimes had trouble reading big words. She reached for his hands and asked, "What if you and I read the Preamble together?" After a brief period of silence, Pace answered, "I'd like that." Barbara and Pace later shared the podium and slowly began reading the Preamble together. When Barbara saw that he was confident in his reading, she stopped reading aloud with him. He finished the Preamble by himself, and the crowd gave him a standing ovation. Barbara gave him a big hug. With her assurance, Pace had triumphed over a moment of difficulty.

The Bushes' road to the White House finally ended in the presidential campaign of 1988. During a presidential campaign, a candidate must surmount endless obstacles— from public indifference to outright hostility—in communicating the message of why the American public should vote for him or her. For those people with presidential ambitions, the pursuit of victory might actually reflect 10 or 20 years of conscious planning and complicated political maneuvering. Jules Witcover wrote in *Marathon*, a book about the 1976 presidential race between Gerald Ford and Jimmy Carter, that running for the office of president "is a grueling, debilitating, and often dehumanizing ordeal that exacts an extravagant price." Not only is the candidate highly visible, but so are family members. They provide a human dimension to the candidate and are a testimony to that candidate's character and values. Each candidate and his or her spouse encounter intense scrutiny as to who best represents what Grimes described in *Running Mates* as "Mr. and Mrs. America."

Barbara Bush and her counterparts were examined by the public almost as rigorously as the presidential candidates themselves, but for different reasons. Barbara emerged into the public arena much more on her own than ever before. She felt the public pressure and admitted to Grimes that "they're laying an enormous load on me, if you want to know the truth. I think that is fair to say."

Over the years the election process has become more and more consuming for the candidates and their families. Although George did not survive the party primaries in his 1980 bid for the presidency, he had gone on to become vice-president. He had eight years to quietly build political and public support for his presidential run in 1988. For the Bush family, the campaign actually began in the spring of 1986, when George gathered the family at Camp David (a woodland camp in the Catoctin Mountains in Maryland that is used by U.S. presidents as a retreat) to ask them for their support. The entire family backed his decision to run, and the race was on.

Unlike state or local campaigns, in which candidates for election exercise a great deal of control, the scale and

The Bushes tour the pyramids in Cairo, Egypt, while on an official trip in August 1986. As the vice-president's wife, Barbara had many opportunities to travel with George on goodwill missions.

complexity of a presidential race necessitates the use of many advisers and consultants for every imaginable aspect of the campaign, from the development, creation, and placement of media publicity to how the candidate dresses and speaks. George himself had been criticized over the years for his uninspiring speaking style and delivery. Barbara also experienced the merciless assessment of political consultants. She received "expert" advice about her hair color, her weight, and her clothing—all of which left her unmoved. Her previous work in George's campaigns was conducted without much fanfare, and little attention was placed on her as an individual. However, with the 1988 campaign, Barbara stepped out of the shadows and into the public eye as never before. Always a dedicated campaigner, Barbara refused to undergo a "repackaging" despite the age and appearance of the other candidates' wives. According to Radcliffe, she informed Bush's media adviser, Roger Ailes, that "I'll do anything you want, but I won't dye my hair, change my wardrobe, or lose weight." Later, in a November 1988 interview with the *Ladies Home Journal* she declared, "I owe it to the public to look nice and have a clean mind and a clean head of hair. And that's it."

Barbara just wanted to look like herself. But some people felt otherwise. They thought her "look" was important, and Barbara called on her reserve of self-deprecating humor to get over the rough spots. Whenever photographers took pictures of her, she joked with them about her wrinkles and how her best smile makes her look like she is being electrocuted. She once told Radcliffe, "My kids are always looking at photographs of me and saying, 'Look at Mom, she's plugged in again!'" On numerous occasions she has felt the sting of being told by the media that she looked more like George's mother than his wife because of her white hair, matronly figure, and weather-beaten skin. During a campaign interview she was once asked by Jane Pauley of NBC's "Today" television show,

"Mrs. Bush, people say George is a man for the eighties and you're a woman of the forties. What do you say to that?" Barbara handled the question with poise and dignity and answered, "If you mean I love my family, my country, and my God, so be it," but despite years of experience in interviewing she later admitted that she had "felt like crying." Throughout the campaign the media raised questions about how Barbara's traditional life-style would appeal to American voters when only about 22 percent could be described as being traditional, that is, as nonworking wives who stayed at home to raise the children. During the Republican primary, Elizabeth "Libby" Dole, wife of presidential candidate Senator Robert Dole of Kansas, also felt the barbs of the media when she resigned her position as President Reagan's secretary of transportation to devote more time to assisting in her husband's campaign. When asked why she had decided to give up her position she responded that she thought women had been struggling for the right to make their own choices, "to do what we feel is right for us." Barbara had always done what she felt was right for her, and that was to be a full-time wife and mother.

George Bush officially announced his candidacy for the presidency on October 12, 1987, in Iowa. Barbara had already visited 42 of Iowa's 99 counties. During the primaries, Barbara traveled around the country with a slide show that depicted what it was like to be the vice-president's wife. She wrote her own script for the slides and described the beautiful places and fascinating peoples she had seen in China and other countries. One anecdote she related to her audience was about how she had once been asked while standing on the receiving line at an evening reception, "Well, who are you?" At the same reception, another guest mistook her for Mrs. George Shultz, the white-haired wife of the secretary of state. Barbara also showed pictures of the vice-presidential house and slides of her children and grandchildren on visits to the family summer retreat in Kennebunkport. She spoke about how much she loved and respected her husband and talked about how she felt he was "presidential" and should have the voters' support. Barbara worked hard to give as many American voters as she could a small glimpse of the public and private lives of the entire Bush family.

Despite the intense campaigning, Bush was beaten in the Iowa Republican primary by Senator Dole and TV evangelist Pat Robertson. Pressure was beginning to mount for the candidates because the New Hampshire primary was approaching. No one who has lost the New Hampshire primary has gone on to be elected president. Before the New Hampshire vote, Bush was scheduled to participate in a debate at Dartmouth College in Hanover, New Hampshire. George's daughter Dorothy later commented to Grimes that as George prepared with his staff for the debate, her mother could not sit in the room and listen. Instead, she went into the next room and worked on her needlepoint, stitching "at about 100 miles per hour."

Bush won the New Hampshire primary and ultimately clinched the Republican nomination on Tuesday, March 8, 1988. In April, Michael Dukakis, governor of Massachusetts, was chosen as the Democratic party's nominee.

After the August Republican Convention in New Orleans, Bush and his family campaigned virtually nonstop. According to an article that appeared in the *Washington Post* two weeks before the election, 63-year-old Barbara Bush and 51-year-old Kitty Dukakis logged in more than 50,000 miles each during 10 weeks of campaigning for their husbands. Kitty Dukakis spent three-quarters of her time campaigning without her husband in 88 cities of 25 states. She had given 900 television, magazine, and newspaper interviews and had appeared at 200 fund-raisers, among other campaign-related events. Dukakis met with photographers and reporters at least 25 times. Her solo schedule became the subject of some debate within the Dukakis campaign, but she felt that it was a waste of time to travel with her husband when she could carry his mes-

sage to even more voters on her own. She told Ann Grimes that she made herself more "vulnerable by agreeing to answer questions. Mrs. Bush chose not to do that, and that's a choice you have to make."

Barbara, on the other hand, was at George's side during about 60 percent of her campaign appearances. She traveled to 92 cities in 29 states, gave 184 television and print interviews, and appeared at 77 fund-raisers and other events. She met with photographers and reporters at 13 press conferences. Barbara had also improved her travel style since the 1980 campaign—she no longer carried her own suitcases, and being the vice-president's wife, she took advantage of having access to the vice-presidential airplane, Air Force Two. Casey Healey, Barbara's personal aide, and Sondra Haley, her press secretary, traveled

Barbara accompanies her husband at a campaign rally in California in November 1988. Barbara, who stumped virtually non-stop for her husband, was at George's side for about 60 percent of her campaign appearances.

with her. Barbara's chief of staff, Susan Porter Rose, worked with the Bush campaign people to plan her appearances. But ultimately Barbara set her own agenda.

Sheila Tate, George Bush's campaign press secretary, later discussed with Grimes how much Barbara had wanted to work for the campaign and how she occasionally felt underutilized, especially when she had to just stand in the background. Barbara asked to be sent on interviews or to do whatever else she could to help. She made visits to schools, Head Start programs, day-care centers, and fundraisers of all types. She even made stops at Republican headquarters to cheer on the campaign workers. She often highlighted the issue of literacy in her appearances. A

Kitty Dukakis, wife of the Democratic candidate for president, Michael Dukakis, answers questions during a news conference in April 1988. Kitty Dukakis spent three-quarters of her time campaigning without her husband and was often drawn into discussing policy issues—issues that Barbara herself refused to comment on publicly.

typical campaign day might include a visit to a Head Start program, followed by a stop at the local Republican party office, then a tour of a school, a stop at a reading program at a housing project, and lunch meetings at two different restaurants. Her limousine, the Secret Service and local police escort vehicles, and press vans made an impressive motorcade, especially in the smaller towns that she visited.

Both Barbara and Kitty Dukakis had to face the steady barrage of reporters' questions throughout the campaign. Unlike Kitty, Barbara steadfastly refused to be drawn into the discussion of policy issues and stayed instead with the subjects of family, literacy, and volunteerism.

Over the years, Barbara has told interviewers that she and George are not demonstrative with their affection for one another in public. They both have a strong sense of propriety. When the issue of how close they were as a couple was raised, Barbara would often describe how much they loved and respected each other, were "best friends," and shared everything.

Barbara gives her son George W. a high five as she arrives at the Republican National Convention in New Orleans. During the 1988 campaign, the press picked up on the public's perception of Barbara's warmth, her down-to-earth personality, her devotion to her children, and her persistence to be herself despite all the campaign pressures.

In the closing weeks of the campaign, the media began to focus even more on Barbara. Crowds responded to her. What had once been called a liability—her white hair—was now deemed a plus. According to Grimes, at a visit to a small town in southern Illinois, a white-haired woman held up a poster that read "White Haired Ladies For Bush!" The woman explained that "I love her self-esteem. She doesn't dye her hair and do all these things. She's so real. I thought I'd encourage her." Another woman who was interviewed acknowledged that although Kitty Dukakis made a good appearance and was well spoken, she respected Barbara because "she sticks by her guns and I don't think she's kissing up to anybody. . . . She is herself and to me that really is her strong point." She also believed that Barbara would not be trying to run "the show from behind the scenes," as many people perceived Nancy Reagan to be doing. Media coverage picked up on the perception of Barbara's warmth, her down-to-earth style, her humor, her devotion to her children and grandchildren, and her determination to be herself despite the campaign pressure.

Behind the scenes, Barbara Bush was a quiet force. After the election, her son Marvin had discussed with Grimes how his mother had become "a little uncomfortable, seeing her husband, whose greatest strength in her eyes is his warmth and his personality, being packaged." Campaign leaks and staff self-aggrandizement made her angry, and she did not hesitate to point out those staffers whom she perceived as ineffective. She was often described as "fierce" in her protection of George and was known to lose her "gracious demeanor" if she felt things were not being handled the way she thought they should be. Throughout the campaign she had knowledge of all developments, but she did not interfere with them. She told Grimes, " 'I listen' and give input 'only if somebody asks, What do you think about that? Or, if I really think something's . . . you know, I might reinforce what someone else says.' "

Bush had experienced defeat in two Senate races and his first run for the presidency. Despite the positive signs of the public opinion polls prior to the election, Barbara was asked in a *Life* magazine interview how she would react to another defeat. She said, "Now I know there is more to life than this. We'll go back to Houston and I'll play with my friends while they can still play, and I want to go down the Intracoastal Waterway [a system of inland waterways along the Atlantic coast, from Cape Cod, Massachusetts, to Brownsville, Texas] with George. You don't have to leap back on the horse and ride the same bucking bronco. I mean, when the race is over, it's over."

On election day, November 8, 1988, the day of reckoning was at hand. After all the years of planning and campaigning, George Herbert Walker Bush was elected the 41st president of the United States, with 54 percent of the electoral vote.

On January 20, 1989, Chief Justice William Rehnquist (right) administers the presidential oath to George as Barbara looks on.

Barbara, wearing a royal blue velvet-and-taffeta dress, and George celebrate at one of the many inaugural balls held in their honor on inauguration day.

7

In the Spotlight

ON INAUGURATION DAY, January 20, 1989, Barbara Bush made her 29th move in 43 years of marriage to George Bush. She and George moved into the White House, at 1600 Pennsylvania Avenue in Washington, D.C., as the president and first lady of the United States. At his swearing-in ceremony, which was held outside on the steps of the Capitol, George spoke about making "kinder the face of the nation and gentler the face of the world" and about the "thousand points of light" who generously volunteered for the good of others. At noon, following the president's speech and the inaugural parade that proceeded down Pennsylvania Avenue, the Bushes hosted a luncheon for 250 relatives. They also made appearances at several inaugural balls that were being held throughout Washington. Grimes relates in *Running Mates* that to one reporter who saw Barbara at their last stop, which was the ball at the Washington Hilton, Barbara was a "hit" at the party in her royal blue velvet-and-taffeta dress designed by Arnold Scaasi and that "all the ladies loved it. They gasped with pleasure when they saw her and pronounced her beautiful."

First Lady Barbara Bush visits residents of a Washington nursing home in 1989. Barbara firmly established her image in the public eye as the standard-bearer of traditional values: devotion to husband and family, service to others, loyalty, good humor, and straight talk.

Barbara had worked alongside George for years to help him achieve the presidency. During the 1988 campaign, she had striven particularly hard to aid him while facing the media's constant attention and the pressure to behave always and only in ways that would reflect well on her husband. After the election, when her campaign work was done, she realized that she faced the very different spotlight focused on a president's wife. The public perception of her as a political helpmate vanished, and she was seen as the first lady of the United States of America, the nation's hostess to the world. Barbara was used to the attention inherent in being the wife of a powerful man, but the amount she received as first lady was unlike anything that had come before. She was presented with a challenge,

for her role as first lady would be in sharp contrast to her customary low profile, which she had maintained throughout the vice-presidential years. Even in 1988 she had almost been chased out of a campaign picture with her husband in San Antonio, Texas, when the photographer failed to recognize her and ordered "the woman in red" out of the photo. Although she had been by George's side for more than 40 years of political life, for the most part she shunned the limelight.

But by the end of the 1988 presidential campaign, she had risen to the challenge and firmly established her image in the public eye as the "Silver Fox," as her children call her. Her white hair, wrinkles, three-strand faux pearl necklace, and grandmotherly aura were instantly recognizable. The American public responded with warmth to what *Time* magazine called her "refreshing new style," and in the first 100 days after George's election, she received 35,000 pieces of fan mail from admirers. Yet her "new style" is based on traditional values: devotion to her husband and family, service to others, loyalty, good humor, straight talk, and acceptance of herself. She has set a style and tone for the White House that not only complements her husband's political agenda but is a true expression of her values.

During the parties and functions of inauguration week, Barbara used her wit and humor to deflect comparisons with the departing first lady. Nancy Reagan was perceived as cool, aloof, and elegant, well known for being proud of her size-four figure and being partial to expensive designer clothing. Barbara, who prefers a completely different style, quickly made that clear by striking a model's pose in front of 6,000 people at an inaugural tribute at the Kennedy Center. She told the crowd: "I want you to look at me. Please notice—hairdo, makeup, designer dress. Look at me good this week, because it's the only week." Actually, Barbara has worn designer clothes for years and joked to Alison Cook, in an interview published in the

The first lady watches Mildred Kerr Bush, called Millie, and her newborn puppies in the White House rose garden..

March 1990 issue of *Ladies Home Journal*, "One of the myths is that I don't dress well. I dress very well—I just don't look so good." Her wit helped her cope with the publicity that comes with being first lady. Almost every move she made was deemed newsworthy. When C. Fred Bush had died on January 20, 1987, George found a new dog for Barbara, which she named Mildred Kerr Bush, after an old friend from Houston. After Barbara moved into the White House, she discovered that even her dog received extensive media coverage. Millie's pregnancy was covered in Washington newspapers, and when she had a litter of six puppies, Barbara and the dogs were featured on the cover of *Life* magazine. The media can seem ubiquitous and even intrusive in the life of a president's family.

Just before Nancy Reagan left Washington, the women of the press who had covered her every move for eight years presented her with a fishbowl to commemorate—and symbolize—the kind of life she had lived in the White House. Now it was Barbara's turn to become, as one reporter put it, the "most watched woman in America." Unlike many first ladies who were thrown into the role with little preparation, Barbara, as the vice-president's wife, had observed Nancy Reagan for eight years. She understood the tremendous responsibilities and pressures that fall to the first lady—what James S. Rosebush referred to in his book *First Lady, Public Wife* as an "unpaid public servant without portfolio." Although Barbara kept a low profile, she avoided much of the media attention, good and bad, that Nancy Reagan had experienced. In her autobiography, *My Turn*, Nancy Reagan discussed some of the unique circumstances that await tenants of the White House. According to tradition, the outgoing first lady takes her successor on a tour of the private rooms of the family residence. Even though the Bushes had visited the White House many times, they had not seen "every nook and hideaway." As Nancy showed Barbara "everything—every closet, every detail from the laundry room on the third floor and the closets where the tablecloths are kept to the beauty parlor that Pat Nixon had installed," she talked about what it was like to live there. She described the challenge of living in a place where 200 people, including guards, household workers, office workers, and others had "passes to our house so you could hardly wear a bathrobe, and you can't walk outside on your lawn."

Americans subject their president and his family to intense examination, much more than do the citizens of other nations. Ann Grimes noted in *Running Mates* that the wife of the German chancellor, husband of the British prime minister, or wife of the French president does not receive nearly as much attention as the first lady. After the 1988 election, Barbara was compared not only to the wives of other politicians but also to previous first ladies—a line that stretches back 200 years. Despite the job's long history, no formal description exists for the position of first lady; no one has established rules for how private or active she should be. In fact, for 100 years after the United States was founded, there was no established form of address for the wife of a president. Abigail Adams, wife of John Adams, whose term extended from 1797 to 1801, was often addressed as Mrs. President and sometimes as Her Majesty. Dolley Madison, who presided over White House functions during the presidency of her husband, James, from 1809 to 1817, was called Lady Presidentess. Not until the inauguration of Rutherford B. Hayes in 1877 was the phrase "the first lady of the land" used to refer to a president's wife. Not all first ladies liked the term. Jacqueline Kennedy suggested it was a good name for a racehorse and preferred not to be called first lady.

When George took on his constitutionally defined duties as president, Barbara shouldered the sometimes nebulous responsibilities of first lady. The undefined nature of the role leaves many Americans ambivalent about it. Barbara was not elected and has no political authority. She cannot be impeached but can and does face criticism for some of her actions. The pressures and demands of the position have affected first ladies in different ways: Abigail Adams said she became "sick, sick, sick, of public life"; Jane Adams, wife of John Quincy Adams, felt like a "bird in a cage"; Julia Grant, wife of Ulysses, recalled her experience as "a bright, beautiful dream." Americans expect their first lady to be gracious, pleasant, and definitely not active in public policy. Barbara's predecessors were subject to pointed criticism at times. For example, when Rosalyn Carter attended meetings of the cabinet, members of the press and public deemed her actions inappropriate. When Nancy Reagan spoke under her breath to President Ronald Reagan to help him answer a question at a news conference, she was reprimanded in the media. Her involvement in the departure of Donald Regan, the president's chief of staff, was greeted with an uproar of disapproval. Margaret "Bess" Truman, wife of President Harry Truman, called the position of first lady "the hardest job in America" because she must show interest in everyone from the farm to the factory, to kings and queens, yet not conflict with her husband's political agenda regardless of

On July 19, 1990, four American first ladies appear together for the first time, in front of the Richard M. Nixon Library and Birthplace at its dedication ceremony. From left to right: Nancy Reagan, Barbara Bush, Pat Nixon, and Betty Ford.

On March 22, 1989, Barbara's volunteer work took her to Grandma's House, a home for infants and small children infected with the AIDS virus, where she held this tiny infant in her arms to show that the disease cannot be spread by casual contact.

her own position. She went on to note that the first lady needs to be nice to the press, no matter how they treat her; dress well, but not overdress; be a devoted wife, but also be independent to a point; and take care of the White House, but not be absorbed by it. Barbara has brought all her experience, personality, and talent to her position and has fulfilled the demands listed by Bess Truman particularly well.

Her long political experience and intelligence helped her avoid some of the publicity problems that Nancy Reagan encountered. Whereas Nancy Reagan was criticized when the public perceived her as spending too much federal money on the White House and its accoutrements,

Barbara has been able to sidestep the issue with her diplomacy. She consistently praised the efforts of Nancy Reagan, claiming that her hard work had saved Barbara trouble. Still, she managed to get what she wanted done without drawing fire. She quietly made a few changes to the family living quarters, such as making offices for George and herself. Ann Grimes quoted an unnamed campaign aide who praised Barbara, remarking: "Barbara Bush changed three or four major rooms up there without any problem at all because she just kept saying she didn't need to change a thing. That is a masterful political way to handle that situation."

Barbara has often said her relationship with George is based on the idea that "I don't fool around with his office and he doesn't fool around with my household." The division of labor has worked well for more than 40 years, but during the early months of the Bush presidency, one of Barbara's forthright comments caused trouble. In mid-January 1989, a gunman equipped with a military assault rifle opened fire in a California schoolyard during recess, killing five children. Commenting on the mass murder, Barbara said in February 1989 that the sale of military assault weapons to private citizens should be "absolutely" outlawed. As the devoted mother of five and grandmother of a dozen youngsters, her reaction was understandable. But the Bush administration endorsed the policy of keeping the sale of automatic military assault rifles legal. The media pounced on the difference between George's policy and Barbara's statement as evidence of dissension in the usually harmonious Bush household. Within days, Marlin Fitzwater, the White House press secretary, announced that there was no disagreement between the Bushes regarding the banning of automatic military assault rifles to private citizens, and while the Bushes traveled on a state visit to Japan, Anna Perez, Barbara's press secretary, stated that the first lady would make no future comments on political issues. Even Barbara's overwhelming personal

Barbara suffers from Graves' disease, a thyroid disorder, but has accepted her condition with good humor. When reporters asked how her eyes were, she responded with this cross-eyed expression.

popularity could not protect her from controversy when she was perceived as entering the sphere of politics.

Barbara soon put the episode behind her and continued to promote volunteer efforts and service organizations. She made the nationwide campaign for literacy more newsworthy just by her endorsement, but her efforts did not stop there. In March 1989 she established the Barbara Bush Foundation for Family Literacy, which helps literacy programs throughout the nation and is supported by private donations. In his December 1988 article in the *Saturday Evening Post*, John Ensor Harr described how Barbara is "universally regarded as the most important national resource the literacy movement has." He attributed her effectiveness to the "totality of her commitment; her personal warmth and depth of understanding; her skill; and above all, her sensitivity to the human dimension."

Despite this image, Barbara noted in a July 10, 1989, *Newsweek* article that her volunteer activities had changed. In the past, she said: "I gave hours of time. And of course, money. Now what I can do best is highlight these programs." Her hands-on involvement has given way to a more symbolic, publicity-oriented approach, but she and George still found time to visit Covenant House, a shelter for runaway teens in New York City, and listen to the residents' stories. Barbara also made a point of visiting a small health-care center in the northwest section of Washington, D.C., called Grandma's House. The center provides services for infants infected with HIV, the virus believed to cause AIDS, and here the press took a photograph of her holding a tiny black baby infected with AIDS. Her visit was sparked by the desire to encourage potential volunteers—to show that the disease is not spread by casual contact. She also continues a few of her personal volunteer efforts; for example, visiting the Ronald Mc-Donald house in Washington, a shelter for seriously ill children receiving specialized medical care in area hospitals. Regarding her new prominence, the persistent scru-

tiny of the media, and their effect on her volunteerism, she told Kenneth T. Walsh in *U.S. News & World Report*, "I don't want to have a light shine on me, but if I do, I want it to shine on someone or something else, too."

During the first few weeks after George's election, Barbara lost a significant amount of weight. She initially claimed it was the stress of living in the White House, but in March she held a lunch with several reporters and announced that the loss was a result of a thyroid disorder called Graves' disease, for which she had begun receiving treatment. The illness is not fatal, but it can make her eyes swell and cause vision problems. However, it has hardly affected her schedule at all. Having Graves' disease occasionally irritates her, but her good humor has helped her cope. When reporters gathered around her after a tennis game at Kennebunkport, Maine, and shouted, "How are your eyes?" she responded by looking straight at a camera, crossing her eyes, and shouting, "They're fine!"

At Kennebunkport, Barbara boils ears of corn for lunch while her son Neil looks on. Despite their full schedules, the Bushes manage to take vacations at their summer home, and whenever possible, the whole family joins them. They enjoy days filled with fishing and playing tennis and golf.

Her schedule as first lady includes a daily swim in the White House pool, several games of tennis a week, and frequent lunches in the White House with her old friends. She entertains the wives of visiting diplomats, answers mail for three or more hours a day, and appears at numerous public functions. For example, when Princess Diana of Great Britain visited Washington briefly one day in October 1990, she joined the Bushes for coffee at the White House. Later that day, Barbara also met with representatives of the NAMES Project to see a panel made for the AIDS Memorial Quilt to honor those who had died of the disease.

Whenever possible, Barbara tries to have lunch with her husband. Occasionally they arrange to have candlelight dinners alone. Barbara has not cooked for more than 10 years; if she and George get a craving for Chinese food, they either order "take-out" or drive to their favorite Chinese restaurant in Falls Church, Virginia, where they order such dishes as Peking duck, orange beef, or Szechuan green beans. Sunday evenings are often spent in the company of friends at informal suppers in the family quarters.

Any semblance of a daily routine, however, is all but eliminated by extensive travel: by the end of 1989, George's first year in office, Barbara had visited 28 cities and 13 different nations. Despite her duties, her devotion to her family remains undiminished. She still particularly loves spending time at the family's summer compound in Kennebunkport, Maine. Every August, Barbara tries to invite the whole family—all 23 members—to visit at once. The days there are filled with boating, tennis, softball, other outdoor sports, and, for Barbara, gardening. Seeing her "grans" (as she calls her growing brood of grandchildren) is very important to her, and she feels that the time at Kennebunkport is a time for them all to "learn a lot about the great worth of family, faith, and friends." She relishes spending time with her children, who have been affected by their father's presidency in different ways.

After the 1988 election Douglas Wead, a former Bush campaign worker, prepared a study on the children of past presidents. Wead investigated the life stories of nearly two centuries of children of presidents, from John Adams, who took office in 1797, to Ronald Reagan. His report identified presidential offspring who had distinguished themselves but also uncovered higher-than-average rates of accidental death, alcoholism, divorce, and a wide variety of personal and financial scandals. Since the ascendancy

In 1989, Barbara, always a good sport, throws out the first pitch at a Texas Rangers baseball game in Arlington, Texas, where the team's stadium is located. George W., the Bushes oldest son, is a managing partner of the team.

On July 11, 1990, Neil Bush takes the stand to defend himself against allegations that he violated banking regulations as director of the Silverado Banking, Savings, and Loan Association. In April 1991, Neil was formally reprimanded by the Office of Thrift Supervision. It is difficult for most presidents' children to stay out of the limelight; both their successes and failures are often criticized by the media.

of television, media scrutiny has seriously eroded presidential family members' sense of privacy and independence, which has also been compromised by the requirements of Secret Service protection. Wead also concluded that almost all their business undertakings are greeted with criticism. Their success is credited to the abuse of family connections; failure is considered the result of stupidity. Charges of grandstanding are leveled at those who involve themselves in political or social causes, and artistic endeavors are labeled self-indulgent by politically active critics. Trying to lead a quiet, normal life, however, may be interpreted as unambitious or lazy. Wead concluded that the best way for a president's offspring to heed his "sobering warning" was to "keep the business mediocre, [and] maintain a personal low profile" in order to ensure relative harmony with the press and the public.

Barbara Kellerman, a political scientist at Fairleigh Dickinson University, evaluated how the Bush family had been treated by the media and concluded, "The decorous image the family represents and Barbara Bush's evocation of traditional, WASP values make people loath to attack them." Yet this reluctance has not completely shielded the children from scrutiny.

Following George's election to the presidency, each of his children has been subjected to far more attention than they had been during the years when George was vice-president. George W.—after Andover, Yale, the air force, and Harvard Business School—launched his career in Midland, Texas, and included oil drilling among his other businesses. Like his father, he is interested in politics. Although he suffered a defeat in his 1978 run for a Texas congressional seat, he worked for 18 months on George's election campaign and transition team. He contemplated a run for governor of Texas in 1990, but his family ties proved to be a hindrance rather than a help. Barbara's advice to him was that he would be in a no-win situation as a son of the president. If the bid succeeded, he would get no personal credit, but if he failed he would get most of the blame.

Barbara has always had a different rapport with George W. than George has had. While George inspires awe in his eldest son, according to an interview Barbara gave Laurence Barrett for *Time* magazine, published July 31, 1989, she and her son fight all the time because "we're so alike.... He does things to needle me, always." Eventually George W. evaluated his position in Texas and decided not to run for governor. In a state sometimes considered sports crazy, he remained prominent in Texas by becoming a managing partner in the Dallas-based Texas Rangers major league baseball team. At his request, Barbara threw out the first ball of the 1989 season. George W. realizes that being the president's son put him in the limelight and admits it has not hurt ticket sales. He signs many autographs at games but recognizes that "it's really not me they want but the President's son, but I can give people a nice memento of visiting the ballpark."

John Ellis Bush, known as Jeb, headed south to Miami to start his career. He too has involved himself in politics, as Dade County Republican chairman and as Florida's secretary of commerce in 1987 and 1988. Jeb is very active in community work and serves on the board of directors of such organizations as United Way and the Children's Home Foundation. He is also an honorary chairman of Miami's Children's Hospital Research Institute Capital Campaign.

Neil Mallon Bush has also depended on his mother's faith and support throughout his life. As a child, his reading disorder made schoolwork difficult, and experts told Barbara he would probably never make it through college. She did everything she could to help him. With the aid of private tutors and hard work, Neil managed to graduate from Tulane University in New Orleans, Louisiana. He headed west to Denver, Colorado, where he become an oil company executive and director of the Silverado Banking,

Savings and Loan Association, the third largest thrift bank in the state. When the bank failed in the late 1980s, the federal government stepped in and negotiated a settlement. The government lawyers concluded that Neil, among others, had violated banking regulations in his actions as director, but he refused to accept a settlement that included such charges. His name appeared frequently in the newspapers, and his brother Marvin angrily spoke to *U.S. News & World Report* in February 1990, claiming, "The focus would not be on Neil Bush today if my dad were not President." In April 1991, Neil was formally reprimanded by the Office of Thrift Supervision, the federal agency that regulates savings and loans associations. In June, Neil and 12 other former directors of the bank agreed to pay the government $49.5 million to settle a civil lawsuit brought by the Federal Deposit Insurance corporation that alleged negligence in the $1 billion collapse of Silverado.

Dorothy Walker Bush, known as Doro, worked as a bookkeeper for her husband's construction company in Maine until she joined the family effort during the 1988 presidential campaign. Following her August 1989 divorce from her husband of seven years, she moved to Washington, where she cares for her two children and has a position as special-events coordinator for the National Rehabilitation Hospital. In a 1988 interview in *McCall's* magazine, she remarked on Barbara's influence: "I often remember things Mother did with me, and I find myself bringing [my children] up the way she brought me up." For Doro, as well as for the rest of her children, Barbara has been an enduring bulwark of support.

As she was when her family was not in the public eye, Barbara is always available to her children to share good times and to help them get through difficult periods. In 1985, she helped Marvin, her youngest son, when he was stricken with a serious chronic disease at the age of 29. That year he was afflicted with ulcerative colitis, a form

of inflammatory bowel disease (IBD) for which there is no known cause or cure. After weeks of hospitalization, he endured two operations to remove his colon and save his life. While Marvin was in the hospital, Barbara spent most of each day with him, and George visited once a day. With his family's support, Marvin made it through and became one of three partners in a small investment firm in Alexandria, Virginia. Barbara is especially proud of the time he devotes to speaking about his disease to those recently stricken with IBD and his volunteer efforts for IBD sufferers.

Throughout her tenure as first lady, Barbara has demonstrated her tremendous appeal to people throughout the country. Many feel that she looks like a person who could

Barbara, her daughter Dorothy, and her granddaughter Ellie LeBlond relax at the White House. Doro, as Dorothy is called, once remarked in an interview that Barbara was a positive influence on her while she was raising her own children.

Barbara tours an adult literacy program at the Bronx Educational Services in New York. Barbara is regarded as an important "national resource" for the literacy movement because of her total commitment to the cause.

be a friend, and numerous interviews stress her down-to-earth personality. But her gracious, self-deprecating style masks the hard work, intensity, and wealth of expertise she brings to every task. Her years of experience as a hostess have left her well equipped to deal with almost any social situation, yet she does not appear overly sophisticated. In her 1990 interview with Alison Cook, Barbara noted: "People write me and say, 'I know I could talk to you.' And they could. And I could talk to them. But I could also talk to the Queen of England. Or maybe I shouldn't use her as an example, but Margaret Thatcher. Or Deng Xiaoping. Or Mrs. Sadat." The quote reveals her as a polished hostess and a cultivated woman self-confident enough not to flaunt her accomplishments.

Her favorite cause, literacy, received a boost when *Millie's Book* was published in 1990. Purportedly dictated to the first lady by Millie, Barbara's English springer spaniel, the book made the best-seller list. Barbara, the actual author, dedicated all her royalties to the Barbara Bush Foundation for Family Literacy. Although such episodes have lightened Barbara's period as first lady, she has also endured stressful times. The months of tension following Iraq's invasion of Kuwait and the subsequent U.S.-led war against Iraq were especially hard for her, because George spent hours with advisers, making decisions that helped ensure the allied victory in Operation Desert Storm. During this tense time, she supported George privately and made a publicized trip on a commercial domestic airline ostensibly to appear at a medical center and air force base but also to reassure travelers frightened by the possibility of terrorism. During Thanksgiving weekend Barbara accompanied the president on a trip to Saudi Arabia to visit U.S. troops stationed there. In addition, as stories and pictures of the war dominated the media, Barbara publicly urged parents to screen what their children saw on television and to help talk them through their fears. She said in a *Washington Post* interview that she became concerned about the dangers of viewing the news programs when three of her own grandchildren, aged four to six, had become upset by the pictures of bombings they had seen on TV while on a visit with her at Camp David. "My kids aren't different than anyone else's," she commented, and "I just think you ought to be careful of your children."

During her time spent as first lady, Barbara has received accolades for her approachable, down-to-earth manner, her sincere dedication to volunteer work, her adroit handling of the media, and her devotion to her family. Her long-standing values are her own, and she has steadfastly stood by her beliefs. The woman who once claimed she thought her major accomplishment would be getting five children through college has succeeded in doing much

President and Mrs. Bush wave to U.S. Marines stationed in eastern Saudi Arabia on Thanksgiving Day in 1990. Throughout Operation Desert Storm, Barbara urged parents to shield their children from the horrors of war that were frequently shown on television and to try to allay their children's fears about what they saw.

more than that. The role of women has changed dramatically since Barbara Bush was a young girl, and the choices she made may not be available to the following generations of women, but the energy and dedication she brought to the trials and opportunities of her life do provide an example for many. Barbara herself seems to have had a fine time so far. In an interview in *Good Housekeeping* magazine, she responded to a question about what she regards as the best time in her life. "Oh, that's easy," she told Jean Libman Block. "It's now, right now. But then, I would have said the exact same thing last year, and the year before, and almost every year before that."

Further Reading

Bush, C. Fred. *C. Fred's Story. Edited slightly by Barbara Bush.* New York: Morrow, 1984.

Bush, George H., and Victor Gold. *Looking Forward: The George Bush Story.* New York: Doubleday, 1987.

Bush, Mildred Kerr. *Millie's Book. As Dictated to Barbara Bush.* New York: Morrow, 1990.

Green, Fitzhugh. *George Bush.* New York: Hippocrene Books, 1989.

Grimes, Ann. *Running Mates: The Making of a First Lady.* New York: Morrow, 1990.

Hyams, Joe. *Flight of the Avenger: George Bush at War.* Orlando, FL: Harcourt Brace Jovanovich, 1991.

Radcliffe, Donnie. *Simply Barbara Bush: A Portrait of America's Candid First Lady.* New York: Warner, 1990.

Reagan, Nancy, and William Novak. *My Turn: The Memoirs of Nancy Reagan.* New York: Random House, 1989.

Rosebush, James S. *First Lady, Public Wife: A Behind-the-Scenes History of the Evolving Role of First Ladies in American Political Life.* Lanham, MD: University Press of America, 1987.

Sufrin, Mark. *George Bush: The Story of the 41st President of the United States.* New York: Delacorte Press, 1989.

Tanner, Louise. *All the Things We Were: A Scrapbook of the People, Politics, and Popular Culture in the Tragicomic Years Between the Crash and Pearl Harbor.* New York: Doubleday, 1968.

White, Theodore. *The Making of the President Nineteen Sixty-Four.* New York: Atheneum, 1965.

Witcover, Jules. *Marathon: The Pursuit of the Presidency, 1972–1976.* New York: Viking Press, 1977.

Chronology

June 8, 1925	Born Barbara Pierce in New York City
1941	Enters Ashley Hall in Charleston, South Carolina, a private boarding school for girls; United States enters World War II; Barbara meets George Herbert Walker Bush
1943	Graduates from Ashley Hall; enters Smith College in Northampton, Massachusetts
1944	Leaves Smith College
1945	Marries George Bush; moves with him to naval training posts in Michigan, Maine, and Virginia; at the end of the war the Bushes move to New Haven, Connecticut, where George enrolls at Yale University
1946	First son, George Walker Bush, is born
1948	Barbara and George move to Odessa, Texas; an early transfer for George sends the Bushes to California
1949	Barbara's mother, Pauline, dies in car accident; Barbara's first daughter, Pauline Robinson Bush, is born
1950	The Bushes move to Midland, Texas
1953	Third child, John Ellis Bush, is born; Pauline "Robin" Bush dies of leukemia
1955	Fourth child, Neil Mallon Bush, is born
1956	Fifth child, Marvin Pierce Bush, is born
1959	The Bushes move to Houston, Texas; sixth child, Dorothy Walker Bush, is born
1966	Barbara helps George in his successful campaign for U.S. House of Representatives seat; the Bushes move to Washington, D.C.
1971	Moves with family to New York City when George is appointed U.S. representative to the United Nations
1973	Moves back to Washington, D.C., when George is named Republican National Commmittee chairman

1974   Goes to Beijing, China, with George when he is named U.S. envoy to the People's Republic of China

1975   Moves back to Washington, D.C., when George is appointed director of the Central Intelligence Agency (CIA)

1977   Moves with George to Houston; helps him prepare for presidential run in 1980; makes national effort against illiteracy the focus of her volunteer activities

1980   Helps George campaign for the Republican presidential nomination; when he is nominated for vice-president, she helps to successfully campaign for Republican ticket

1984   *C. Fred's Story*, a book about the life of her pet spaniel, is published; Barbara donates all profits to literacy efforts; helps in landslide reelection win of the Reagan-Bush ticket

1988   Assists George in his successful campaign for president

1989   Moves into White House as first lady; establishes Barbara Bush Foundation for Family Literacy

1990   *Millie's Book,* a book about the life of Barbara's dog in the White House, is published and becomes best-seller; Barbara dedicates all royalties to her literacy foundation

1991   Flies on commercial airliner to demonstrate safety of air travel during Operation Desert Storm; visits U.S. troops in Saudi Arabia; continues to promote literacy and volunteerism

Index

PICTURE CREDITS

Arleen McGrath Heiss is a graduate of Mount Holyoke College and has a masters of public administration degree from American University. A freelance writer, she is also a management consultant specializing in organizational development. She has worked as a volunteer in such areas as women's education, cancer research, and community and youth organizations. She has been a volunteer for Mrs. Bush's office in the East Wing of the White House. Ms. Heiss lives in Washington, D.C., with her husband and two children.

Vito Perrone is Director of Teacher Education and Chair of Teaching, Curriculum, and Learning Environments at Harvard University. He has previous experience as a public school teacher, a university professor of history, education, and peace studies (University of North Dakota), and as dean of the New School and the Center for Teaching and Learning (both at the University of North Dakota). Dr. Perrone has written extensively about such issues as educational equity, humanities curriculum, progressive education, and evaluation. His most recent books are: *A Letter to Teachers: Reflections on Schooling and the Art of Teaching*; *Enlarging Student Assessment in Schools*; *Working Papers: Reflections on Teachers, Schools, and Communities*; *Visions of Peace*; and *Johanna Knudsen Miller: A Pioneer Teacher*.